Low Explosions

Low Explosions

WRITINGS ON THE BODY

EDITED BY CASIE FEDUKOVICH
WITH STEVE SPARKS

A publication of the Knoxville Writers' Guild
KNOXVILLE, TENNESSEE

THE KNOXVILLE WRITERS' GUILD
P.O. Box 10326
Knoxville, TN 37939-0326
www.knoxvillewritersguild.org

Book design by Travis Gray @ Robin Easter Design
www.robineaster.com

Table of Contents

Introduction

A **SHRINE BOTH** ancient and modern, the human body remains a site of warfare, lovemaking, nation building, peace making, religious fervor, and personal reflection. From The Venus of Willendorf to Venus Williams, tribal weight-gain rituals to Weight Watchers, humans are fascinated by their own bodies—its functions, purposes, and structure—and by the bodies of those around them. From size and shape to skin color, pregnancy, aging, ailments, disabilities, extra-abilities, disorders and genetic composition, this book peeks inside some of the most commonly fought yet controversial battles raging inside the human body.

Ironically, this basic "common ground," that each person has a body and can articulate life inside that body, serves as the single most divisive issue in contemporary life. Anytime we "modern" humans mount our cultural high horses, we should remember that, long before plastic surgery, all-night gyms, racial profiling, and spray-on tans, societies much less "civilized" than ours worshipped their own culturally-constructed "perfect" bodies. How would ancient fertility goddesses consider Americans' obsession with saddlebags? Civilizations define their mores through their conceptions of the body: Pottery bordered with lithe Egyptian forms. Lush Matisse nudes seductively reclining. "Scientific" descriptions of the "Hottentot Venus." Dorothea Lange's stark, black-and-white "Migrant Mother" photographic series. Current debates on "educational segregation." Far removed from any artificial designation of time or place, we can't escape the pervasive influence of what some scholars call "body politics" on our psyches and, in turn, their effects on our daily actions. We inherit our preoccupations with the body from these histories of paradoxical worship and punishment, while spicing them with Western culture in general, American culture in specific, and southern culture in ultra-specific. So the parts that were once worshipful—such as the exaggerated hips and breasts of the Venus of Willendorf—are now, through our cultural lens, undesirable, and even cause disruptions like eating disorders.

The cultural baggage of this volume intimidated me. In addition to the voyeuristic nature of editing, this book offered a tapestry of experience that resonated far beyond geographic borders. The Guild invited writers to tell stories of and about their bodies, and the products were so graceful—or so brutally brilliant—that choosing among the work became nearly impossible. Whether the experiences described were lived or imagined, I found that the same conversations occurred miles—even countries—apart. Women in London worry about the size of their thighs just like women from Brooklyn or Portland or Knoxville. Men in Canada contemplate sexual fitness just as deeply as men from New Orleans or California. Racial and ethnic tensions occur in urban centers and rural pastures alike, and writers from sea to sea worry about age spots and wrinkles. As the submissions poured in—and I stopped counting at 500—it surfaced that, while the same struggles took place the world over, each experience bore the mark of its creator. In the end, deciding among these visceral self-portraits became one of the toughest tasks I've faced. How could I choose the "best" writing in a pool that included so many moving tales? The decisions were hard, but I am confident that the authors inside present some of the best writing that East Tennessee—and points beyond—has to offer. These powerful pieces reclaim the individuality of the human voice while engaging in a vivid dialogue on the cultural, political, and personal place of the body in the modern world, which too often homogenizes human experience. The stances are as varied as the authors; many indict modern media for pushing unattainable cultural standards, some look to the past to find understanding in the present or to puzzle through historical events, and each presents truth, beauty, and fluid reflective writing on the place of the human body right now, in time, where we are. Even the more fictive works call on common human experience to bring the audience to their respective places.

Many authors choose to set their bodies among the mountains of Tennessee, and, in these pieces, the landscape of the mind intermixes with the natural landscape so seamlessly that the two are indistinguishable. The personal becomes political in those pieces dealing with issues of race, gender, class, sexual orientation, socioeconomic status, and ethnicity to remind us that the playing field, though improved, is still far from level. All of the pieces contend with some major explosion, whether actual— heart attacks and orgasms—or metaphorical—the author's realization that he or she is "that age" or "that weight" or "that color." Explosions, on any scale, are disruptive, but many of the pieces inside move beyond the initial eruption of body, mind, or spirit to bring the reader to a quiet and satisfied end. I can only hope that the collection itself mirrors this graceful arc.

To construct this body of work from so many disparate bodies, for me, echoed the sentiments found in the pieces on pregnancy and childbirth. First the anticipation of the project overwhelmed me. *This book will tell the stories of generations!* Then came the fear and anxiety about proper process. *Am I feeding the book what it needs to grow? What if it reads more like a Picasso nude than a Matisse?* Now, I feel this volume has traveled from conception to creation and emerged on the other side full-bodied and vital. The authors and visual artists inside have honored us with their gifts; I honor them with this volume.

— *Casie Fedukovich*
Knoxville, Tennessee

Acknowledgements

The Knoxville Writers' Guild Anthology relies on generous financial support from local businesses. The profits from the sell of these books fund workshops and monthly programs produced by the KWG. The Guild is a non-profit organization that serves and encourages East Tennessee writers of all levels, and we rely on help from local agencies. The following businesses support the arts—and the artists—in East Tennessee. Without their financial contributions, this volume would not be published.

The Clayton Family Foundation
Pilot Corporation
Kimberly-Clark
The East Tennessee Foundation
The Tennessee Arts Commission
Brian Conley
The Hodges Better English Fund, English Department, University of Tennessee

As with any multi-phase project, this book wouldn't be possible without selfless and skilled volunteers. Their sharp eyes, warm personalities, and dedication to detail enrich *Low Explosions*. I would like to sincerely and emphatically thank Maegan Carr, Carolyn Corely, Mark Estrada, Heather Gravett, James Johnston, and Lindsey Rae for their time, effort, and intelligence. They worked for chocolate and expressed "excitement" with tasks like proofreading. Never before have I worked beside such fun, responsible, and skilled people.

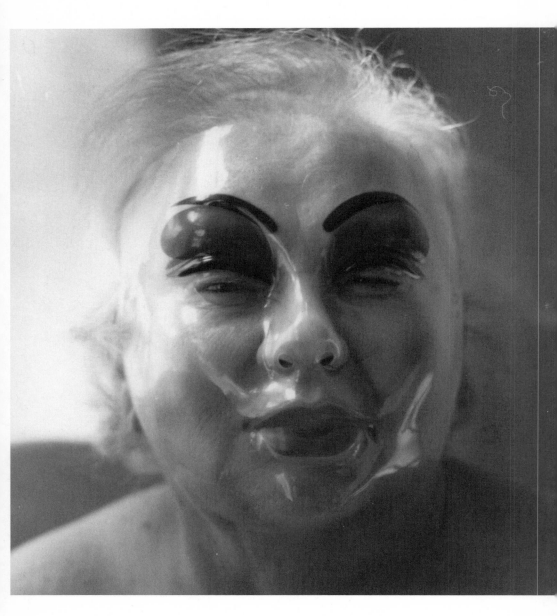

BERNIE IN TRANSPARENT MASK
Richard Remine

"I exist as I am, that is enough."
Walt Whitman
Poet

"The human body is not a thing or substance, given, but a continuous creation. The human body is an energy system which is never a complete structure; never static; is in perpetual inner self-construction and self-destruction; we destroy in order to make it new."
Norman O. Brown
Philosopher

"The most beautiful words in the English language are not 'I love you,' but 'it's benign.'"
Deconstructing Harry
American Film

SOUTHERN GIRL (DETAIL)
Karley J. Sullivan

ANDES

Stephen Mead

Of your ankles,
Mouth's view down here where
A country of cats chasing crickets &
Drop cloth impressions for paintings
Are the horizons our tenderness contours...

This floor, this studio, Autumn time
With not a thing as sunset clear
But the light's white tang
Suffused with the whole range
Of yellow's spectrum
Against knees sloping up &
The plateaus of calves &
Ribs as a boat
My probing nose nudges
As life itself is nudging us:

Live this. Live this now.

RIVER GODS

Jesse Graves

I've stood beneath this bridge before.

Dreaming my way back into seven-year-old eyes,
eruptions of fireworks flare into the Labor Day air
and cascade brilliantly down to the dark waves.

In the time-lapse of remembering, my life
folds back through the warp of this city
the way the Tennessee River winds through it,

and I live again on the north bank, in Maplehurst,
watching the slow seep of barges downriver,
leaving Holston Gaslines for some western port.

Years break apart, become sediment in the stream
of those distant days, their blue-lobed nights.
Twenty-two and alive only to feel.

Still, I dared it only once, walking the trestle where
Sut dragged his trolling line for catfish to sell
on the Square in Cormac McCarthy's hillbilly *Ulysses*.

Who would care to do such a thing alone?
So J.D. and I left our notebooks open on the bank
stepped out a hundred feet over the night.

We sprang from tie to tie, hoping for solid wood,
for no rumbling from beyond the south hill,
our veins soldered by a half-litre of Maker's Mark.

Held aloft by the confluence of blind river gods,
above the circulations of ancient, whiskered fish,
so much of the unknown rushing beneath us.

Mama Heat

Katherine Frank

Nothing's better than crawling into a winter
Bed with my bone-aching husband who
Asks me to spoon him and turn on my
Mama Heat.

Whenever my toddler son snatched
Dog food and ran wild in wet grass,
I'd fold his cold, twittering bones next to mine,
Close my eyes, hum and whisper,
And concentrate on making my baby warm.

No one who knew me as a shivering child
Could foresee hugs and heat in my future.
My family dodged touching, warm or cold;
My skeptical lawyer brothers believe
Ice and blood are interchangeable elements,
But body heat became my response for
Childhood disease, blue-frosted fingers, and bad news.

I tell the doubters it's all in the heart:
Love somersaults out from heaven within.
King David bade Abishag, a woman from a resting place,
Lie next to him and warm his aging blood.
Now, when I see frescoes of Mary and baby Jesus,
Haloes sparkling, I think:
Mama Heat.

FOR THE PATRIOTIC WOMAN HE COULDN'T COME HOME TO
Askhari

He saved stories to tell you. Yesterday,
he was sand stepping
his way west with
more baggage than he could bear.

Now, he is:

one head, no dreds
    two feet, ten frozen toes
    almost unarmed
    southpaw, swollen trigger finger
    half heart
    one open eye
    eardrums, both busted
one mouth, missing tongue.

Go ahead girl.

Get on with flag flying and
ribbon tying
but, even with an atlas

you will not find him.

CIRCULATION
Emily Thompson

THE APARTMENT I share with Jamelah is quite literally crooked. The living room is higher than the bedroom, and when I peer in at Jamelah while she does her reading or listens to music, I feel, even ever so slightly, that I am peering at her from some great distance. And when I splash dishwater onto the floor, it trickles downward, from the kitchen to our front door. We're used to all this now, to the way the washer shakes and tumbles somewhat downhill from its original standing point; it jiggles and jumps as it washes our clothes. I've grown used to the clothesline, too. It hangs over a canal, yawning and stretching all the way to its hook on the *Arsenale* building, some fifteen yards from our crooked window. I'm used to the wind and the rain, and I no longer hang my underwear or socks on the line. Jamelah hasn't taken the hint, and sometimes Stephania from downstairs knocks to return her lonely garments, fallen soldiers. Or sometimes these socks, underwear, bras—all too big to be mine—land in the canal where they slowly drown, if they aren't poisoned to death by filth and gasoline and disease first.

* * *

I keep an ongoing list of oddities I see in the canals, items that don't belong there but are there nonetheless as I hurry past them on my walks to school, or to the rizzo pane, or to the bars. Shoes, a book, an entire pizza, a dead cat. *Gatto*, I said as I ran past. *Gatto morto*.

My ongoing list of canal obscurities hangs on the cupboard above the kitchen sink. The list is crooked, but only because I hung it that way. This morning, Jamelah used a blue marker to add our eighteenth item, *some guy's vomit*, because last night we watched a stranger hit his knees and puke into the canal outside Café Blue. Filth and disease, that's all the canals really are.

* * *

In Detroit, a little boy on the bus asked Jamelah what she was. *A lady*, she said, but that, of course was not the answer the little boy was looking for. He said he thought she might be One of Those Mexican Italians. He was four, maybe five, and his mother or sister or aunt slapped his knee, and he shied away, embarrassed and sorry. For Jamelah, identity is a common misunderstanding, but she fits in well here, in Venice—olive skin and black hair and oversized breasts. I am the blonde; I am the one whose hair everyone wants to grab and pull. I am called *Bianca Nevica*, Snow White. Stranger. But even so, I am more at home here than Jamelah, the tourist. I *am* a stranger; this fact is my comfort.

* * *

Nights when I do not study at cafes or drink at bars, I sit on the lawn furniture in our crooked apartment and listen to Jamelah talk to on the phone, talk across time zones, to her mother, her boyfriend, her sister. She twirls her hair in her pointer finger and recounts the days: *we learned a new verb form*, or *we saw the Tintorellis*. This, our life here, is for Jamelah a semester abroad. She will pack everything in, and she will get back on a plane and go back home.

I do not call my mother to tell her about the museums or the verbs because I do not want to tell her what she does not want to hear. After this is over, I am not coming home.

* * *

Everywhere I go, I hurry. I am a runner; hurrying is my pastime. I am quick, but not neglectful. I know the importance of seeing. I run; I cross bridges to *Salute* and *Ca'Rezzonico* and *San Silvestro*, my favorite churches, my favorite buildings. I turn corners until the scents of *rizzo panes*—sweet and salty, and warm, and new breads—get into me. I stop to take inventory at vegetable stands, catch my breath, go on. It helps, as I cross the bridges, to plan meals to make for Jamelah, something to look forward to. I run, weave my way through the traffic of tourists, and run on. To *Ferrovia*, where I watch the trains come in, listening to the skidding sound of steel on steel. The chaos of travelers, coming and going. This is a comfort. I run; we are all lost.

At the *Academia* bridge, I am halfway home. I stop at the top and watch the boats come in from the *Lido*. Count the boats, keep running. My pulse beats into sidewalks, networks through the cracked stone, meets me again a few strides down the path. Sometimes, I do not know where I am going, but I keep running.

* * *

As often as possible, I pay the museum fee to cross the Bridge of Sighs, the bridge named for the last sounds Venetian prisoners made as they were led from their cells and to their deaths. Three, four times a week—I cannot get enough of it. I cross the bridge, and I stop and gaze out at all those thousands of tourists taking pictures of what I am inside. I am inside history. I cross the bridge feeling what it might be like to *be* a prisoner. And I feel the echoes of the past, the vibrations of bodies and brains which died, which were born only to die, those echoes which have been resonating since creation. I cross the bridge, and I head to my apartment, free.

* * *

I watch the boats—they sway back and forth, triumphant on the water—and I feel like I am drowning.

At the end of the year, Jamelah will pack for home, carefully wrapping her souvenirs, her gifts for her mother, her material memories. When we travel, shop or wander, I don't purchase much; frankly, I don't want the baggage. Jamelah knows I'm not going back; she asks what I'll do, and I tell her the truth. I don't know.

I'll stay in Venice and continue running. I'll stay out of the canals. I'll head south to Tuscany, get work in an olive orchard. I'll pick olives, roll them between my hands, look to the sky, move on. I can go to Scotland or Ireland, get wet when it rains somewhere in a green and rolling valley. I'll hop on a plane for New Zealand, Bali, or Singapore. Afterwards, I'll work on a river in Belize. I'll let the water run over my feet, and I'll remember that my home is here. Anywhere. Nowhere.

Or I will go to Wyoming, Utah, or Idaho. I will disappear into the dust and re-circulate in the thin, sweeping air.

Paying Attention

Connie Jordan Green

The woman behind the counter
  closes her fingers around each box,
    each bag of fruit.
The carton of eggs,
  jug of milk
    glide over the glass surface,
beep to the cash register,
  to the computer that counts inventory,
    to a screen the customer views.
The woman's rooted feet support legs,
  hips that sway oh so slightly
    to the dance of her hands—

reach, lift, swipe, set aside,
reach, lift, swipe, set aside.

For these eight hours her arms
  forget the weight of a baby,
    press of his head against her shoulder,
smell of just-washed hair,
  wisp of sour milk breathed into her neck.
    Her heart beats with the bar-code scanner,
while its echo for nine months
  sings a steady song to other ears,
    falls asleep to the dance of other hands.
Each can of corn, sack of flour

weighs like silver—another paycheck,
food, shelter, clothing—

she pays attention
to the work of her hands.

Nipples

Kelly Falzone

God holds us,
hands around our ribcage,
almost breaking-open
bread.

Setting us into life
those hands lift away
leaving drifts like meringue
in two peaked places:

the rosy-dark thumbprints
of God.

✳

The Woman in the Red Bikini

Lucy Sieger

I FELT EVEN MORE tense than usual. Maybe it was because her breasts were spilling out of her bikini top, errant nipples threatening to escape to daylight, right in front of dozens of sunbathers.

My husband and I were on our annual beach vacation in Wild Dunes, South Carolina. We'd set up camp in the sand, in our formulaic way. Umbrella angled just so; chairs to either side; cooler with water, beer, and wine planted between us; sunscreen applied to every crevice. I sat down, inhaling and exhaling to dissipate my omnipresent anxiety. Relax, I told myself, you have exactly one week to unwind.

Sipping on a glass of wine helped. So did deep breathing, but then I saw *her*. She was a weathered 35 or a youthful 45, who knew. She was overweight, not obese, but her round belly was more in place in a Renoir painting than on a twenty-first century beach. Curly brown hair frothed over her shoulders, pert face, but yes, she was chunky. And scandalous, for she was wearing a tiny red bikini, which cut into her generous flesh. I winced at the fashion *don't*.

But she didn't look like she was in pain, or even self-conscious. In fact, she was enjoying herself! She and her husband played a raucous game of paddleball, and I was transfixed. She whooped and hollered, swooping for the ball, tiny red triangles barely containing her voluptuousness. She dived into the sand, breasts swayed, legs splayed, heavy thighs curdled with cellulite.

How dare she? I gaped, nursing my wine. Such uninhibited movement in any female over age nine, let alone a plump one, was disconcerting. And here I was, body mass index a good five points lower than hers, sidelined like an awkward teenager at a dance. Planted in the safety of the beach chair was my well-exercised bottom, covered by a discreet, skirted bathing suit.

The woman in the red bikini was possessed. She romped, she frolicked, she flaunted her flawed body with abandon. As the paddleball game continued, I became more obsessed with her background. Was she raised on a freewheeling Polynesian island? The French Riviera? Perhaps she grew up in a loincloth and lei, the child of a paradise never penetrated by the notion of womanly figure as original sin.

Surely, she couldn't be a product of my culture. I began dieting 30 years ago, and I'd not felt comfortable in a bathing suit since I was a pre-pubescent girl. I listened carefully for her foreign accent, but the guffaws and shrieks that wafted over the ocean breeze were thoroughly American.

I noticed my husband watching her, too. She was sexy—this woman who didn't do purgatory at the gym, who enjoyed the warmth of the sun on as much skin was legally permissible, who relished her Krispy Kreme donuts. I envisioned her eating one with finger-licking gusto, a crème-filled pastry, custard oozing out of the dough much as she was oozing out of her bikini. She was like a flapper who'd discarded her Victorian corsets for freedom—freedom to exist in her body, freedom to be sensual.

I thought about three decades of commiserating with girlfriends about our weight, our flawed figures. Who were we trying to be so perfect for, anyway? Our boyfriends, our husbands? Any man would find my red-bikinied goddess, footloose and fleshy in the sand, much more appealing than me, with my rigid thighs and locked knees and god-awful skirted bathing suit. For a moment, I felt sorry that my husband couldn't go off and experience this woman, for if she were that much fun on the beach, imagine what she'd be like behind closed doors.

But that's my same old competitive mentality, I realized. I got the feeling this woman didn't analyze who her body would pleasure or who it would threaten. She was too busy enjoying the luxuries it offered *her*.

I wish I could say the woman in the red bikini transformed my life. That I said to hell with it, stopped jogging, threw out the scale, started eating donuts, and took up paddleball. It was not to be. What she did, instead, was provide a glimpse of possibilities.

Imagine, she whispered. Imagine if the river of angst and unhappiness you and your sisters poured into your bodies were redirected down a different channel—one of desserts, shrieks and laughter, of a lusty game of paddleball on a hot summer day. Imagine if you passed this on to one other woman, and she did the same, and so on...

Like a tiny sapling piercing the shell of its seed, this radical concept is taking root inside of me.

Parts

Laura McCoy

That your eyes were my blue ocean
   And your lips my tallest ship;
happily would I sail you
eastern tongue to western hip.

WORTH THE RISKS

Matt Urmy

she sits in her chair by the table and lamp,
I sit beside her drawing table.

we talk, smoke cigarettes,
drink espresso with rice milk.

as she gets up to go out
I kneel in front of the chair

and lean into her chest, kiss her neck,
and slide my hands around her lower back.

she allows this and gently pulls her fingers up
and down my spine. I know what I'm doing

is killing a tiny part of our togetherness.
then she walks out into the night's streets

and I happily allow this,
hoping it's the things that die

in this world that can
live in us the longest.

Vulcan's Vase: Shedding Skin

Billie Nelson

I dream of Vulcan's hands
not muscular—
not the ones that forged
Achilles' shield
but soft and supple.
The ones that caressed
Pandora awake.
Vulcan's tendons
form ridges as clay squishes
between thin fingers and the vase emerges.
This time Vulcan shapes me from clay.
Body warmth mixes with my cold surface.
Muddy water glides away as his hands
reach under my skin
even the walls
smooth my lip outward.
Vulcan leans closer,
rubs away dry skin.

Lazarus Time

Kim Frank

I'm in a Lazarus cycle:
puffy cysts fill up like teenaged
boilish pox heads ready
to pop & kill my baby-faced charm.

Fungus eats every sweaty crease.
My feet's swellin, worried about
haulin me to the fridge discolored,
pickled, veiny, sweet dill stinky.

My eyes are yellowy, but I ain't
Sick—not traditionally. Maybe
it's corrupted humors.
The cokes & coffee don't help.
I drink a lotta milk.
Everything bad tastes good to me.

Doc says I gotta bring it down.
He's bleedin my neck with leeches,
& they're suckin my HMO dry.
Doc thinks I'm too goddamned
lazy to exercise, but even
if I was perfect, would
I live forever? I
doubt it. I doubt almost everything.

Subway

Karley J. Sullivan

❋

The Corner of Freud and Gay

Julie Auer

Tonight, Gay Street is a tableau vivant of small-town cheer wound up in big-city bustle. In the frigid air of early December, crowds are packed in tight between curbs and the renovated facades of historic downtown Knoxville. Upper-level windows glow in warm gold tones against the frosty dusk outside, and shadowy figures obscured by antique glass posture themselves for a view of the busy street below, filled with weary mothers fastening their children's jackets at the neck and making sure the hoods cover tiny ears, and fathers raising delighted toddlers onto their shoulders.

I'm not in a particularly good mood at the moment, though. I didn't know the damned Santa Parade was going on tonight when I made plans to join friends for a drink at the Bistro, which has been closed for a private party, and I've just found out from a cell phone call that the meeting has been moved to a bar in the Old City. So I not only have to walk in thirty-degree cold the length of South Gay Street to Jackson Avenue and all the way down to Manhattan's, I have to push past a few thousand parents who have staked out their territory and jealously guard it against impatient interlopers just trying to cut through to Happy Hour.

Well, TGIF, everybody. I'm going to get my buzz on. I've had a rough day of looking and feeling forty. The morning began with a fierce battle between my tweezers and a stubborn chin hair that I believe in earnest is rooted in the bone and supported by a vast and sinister network of subcranial hair follicles implanted in my brain and programmed to drive me into pre-menopausal insanity. I had a hard time finding my tweezers, too, and wondered vaguely if they were deliberately hiding, determined to avoid another humiliating duel with the whisker.

I always get the bastard in the end, but today it took me longer than ever, and it made me contemplate other flaws, like the frown lines that probably wouldn't be set as deep if I spent less time harpooning my chin. But I smiled at my tired features this morning, grinned wickedly at those frown lines, in fact, because I knew that in three weeks, a dermatologist was going to stab them with a paralyzing toxin. When Botox comes into my life, I'll be able to look that chin hair coldly, without evident emotion, like a mule staring down a carrot. The whisker will be rattled by this stony countenance, and will yield, even to my emasculated tweezers.

The thought of that upcoming victory fuels my stride, and I lope toward Jackson Avenue more brazenly against the crush of parade gazers. I cross Gay Street, and then Summit Hill, where the parade route cuts off. The 100 block of Gay teems with my people, the downtownies: club cronies, bar bitches, and gallery geeks. The Emporium is hosting some sort of jewelry and craft show. As I breeze by, I glance inside and notice the usual arty suspects strolling about in their black turtlenecks and fey postures, glasses of red wine in hand. I notice how trendy the boxy black eyeglass rims have become.

I pause for just a few seconds at the plate glass window of the Emporium. Aw, look at the cute hip young women. They're so supple in their low-slung jeans and slinky silky shirts with lacey spaghetti straps, and as if to spite the weather and boast their nubile sexuality, they're not wearing jackets. Their eyes gleam, unadulterated by even the merest makeup, porcelain cheeks blush as they smile; hair is cropped or falling down on bare, white shoulders. They're so pretty. So young. So unaware of the horror of their future. One day, those dainty eyes will crackle with every wince of crusty crow's feet, and they'll spend hours of resistance training keeping the forces of teacher arm at bay. Meanwhile, I stare hungrily at those lithe young arms until I catch the eye of one of the lovely hipsters, and I realize my nose is pressed against the glass, and I look like a late-model kid ogling my favorite toys in the department store Christmas display. She smiles honorifically, the way you look at a war veteran riding in the back of a convertible in a parade.

Beauty bounces me back on my course, and as I round the corner of Gay and Jackson, I encounter a very large woman wearing a clown suit and smoking a cigarette standing in an alcove of the Jackson side of the Emporium. A light bulb hanging in the alcove is shorting out, giving off a weird strobe illumination of her, and as I glance at her, I notice the car- toonish makeup on her face is streaked. A crying, obese clown lady. I feel like I'm in an Italian movie. Maybe if I backtrack to Gay Street and cut across Wall Avenue to Market Square, I'll find an Anita Ekberg look-alike drenched in the fountain, with swain Marcello Mastroianni in felt hat and boxy black rims marveling at her voluptuous gaiety.

Probably not, I decide. It's December, it's thirty degrees, and the foun- tain is closed for the season. And this is Knoxville. My beloved city is, for better or worse, less *La Dolce Vita* and more *La Strada*, and the grieving clown lady is as close to the world of Fellini as I'll come tonight. I vaguely wonder what has made the girl so sad. Perhaps she feels silly wearing a clown suit. Maybe people have laughed at her, and she wonders deep down if it's the clown suit, her clownish antics, or something else they're laugh- ing at. Maybe their laughter is a reverberation of her bitter amusement at herself, at her looks, at her great height and extravagant weight, the large features made more outrageous by bright-colored face paint. Even though I only glanced at her, I noticed the way the pale pancake makeup and purple glob of lipstick highlighted the yellow of her teeth as she smiled wanly at my terse hello, at the way her tear had taken an alternate path to the made-up tears painted in green and red.

I pad along Jackson's dark cobblestones and clench my teeth against barely perceptible tears forming in my own eyes as wind-whipped cold knifes my face and makes my ass break out in goose bumps. I hear a clink and instinctively glance into the alley leading through a parking lot to Summit Hill. The tin laughter of a scrawny young dude wearing a toboggan directs my view to a wall with freshly sprayed graffiti. The boy is bending over to pick up the can of spray paint he has dropped. He's silent for a mo- ment as he stands up to regard his work, and then he chuckles again, and I gather he's stoned on something, maybe the paint. The roar of a truck, pulling a float up Summit Hill, tumbles through the alley, and the vague beam of distant headlights pans across uneven black letters splashed over an old mural: *Fuck Art. Let's Kill.* How derivative, I think. What's the point of being young and scornful if you can't at least be original? The thought then occurs to me that he's a born critic, and will one day be sporting a goatee and a black turtleneck at somebody else's art opening.

A few seconds later, I arrive at Manhattan's, the bar I like to think is named after the bittersweet cocktail. Ah, just on the other side of that door, there is warmth. I can feel its soft glow already, and smell the hardwood of those creaky old saloon floors. Before the door, however, stands a man of great height, with wide shoulders and a pelt of thick white hair and matching beard. His eyes are like lumps of smoldering coals stuck in the sockets, and he stands with his mighty arms folded.   He glowers at me, then suddenly smacks one massive paw against the door, throwing it open for a crush of partygoers whirring past me into the bar. An orange glare of light and warmth floods over me; confetti of throaty cackling and cheery banter tickles my ears. The door flumps shut again, and the polar bear tucks his paw back in the arm fold.

"I'm expected inside," I tell him. "May I get by you?"

He shakes his head and stands with his legs wide apart.

"I'm expected inside," I insist.

He says nothing, but stares at me gravely. A young couple rounds the corner and steps up to the door. The bear opens the door for them, and it occurs to me that there is another private party going on, but how does the bear know I'm not invited?

I feel pathetic asking, "Is it because of the way I look?"

He resumes his stance and looks over my shoulder.

"College party? Kids, right?" I guess out loud. "I've been in there before. How dare you keep me out?"

No words. He stands before me like a statue. I want to stab him. I want to run past him and kick in the door, just to show him I can do it. I've belonged inside there before. How can you belong somewhere one day and be denied entry on another?

"I'll pay you," I say desperately. "By God, I'll give you money; just let me inside there for two minutes."

A hand withdraws from his armfold and covers his mouth as he yawns. Staring straight ahead.

"Oh, you're a cold devil," I say. Defeated, I turn back.

I'm pacing along Jackson Avenue, toward the cobblestone rise, when I spot the old man whose profile is as familiar to me as the ghost of any of my antiquated heroes. There on the crest of the hill stands the figure of Sigmund Freud silhouetted against the lamp-lit mist of Gay Street, lighting a cigar and regarding me with a sidelong glance as he tosses his match to the ground. I stop in my tracks and gaze at the elegant coat, hat, cigar: the whole form of Freud cut in shadow.

We stare quietly at each other for a moment from a distance of several yards. Horns and cymbals of marching bands echo through the mist, as do the laughter and cheers of the distant crowd. Clouds of breath issue from my parted lips. Finally, I speak.

"They won't let me in."

In his calm, accented English, Freud says, "Who won't?"

"The bouncer at Manhattan's," I say, pointing my thumb over my shoulder, "and all those young little bastards inside."

"Youth has rejected you?"

I scowl at him. "Are you saying you think I look old?"

"I'm asking you how you perceive their rejection."

"I'm forty," I say emphatically. "And I still live as though I were 25. Shouldn't I be settled down by now?"

"You've had plenty of opportunities," he reminds me.

"Yes," I reply irritably, jabbing my index finger into my forehead. "Each one of them etched in my forehead like rings in a tree trunk. Or hey, I've got a better metaphor. The face of a woman is a tapestry of emotional bondage weaving in new threads with each passing year." I smile with pride at my fancy utterance.

He puts one hand in his coat pocket and holds his cigar in front of him with the other. "Bondage," he repeats. "How long have you been using that word?"

"Not long enough for it to mean anything peculiar," I say.

"Do you find yourself fantasizing about straps or leather masks?"

"I only just used that word the first time tonight!" I sputter. "Stop missing my point!"

"What is your point?"

I hiss, "I'm over the *hill*."

"Yes, of course. And there are other hills to climb." He puts the stem of his pipe against his lips and draws smoke.

Suddenly, two young women pass me from behind, arm in arm. Chattering about something, they don't seem to notice me. They hop into a car parked next to a warehouse, and within a few seconds, the car has sped down Jackson Avenue, into the Old City and out of sight.

Freud appears to be staring at me, waiting for a response. I avoid his gaze and glance in the direction of where the young women have gone. Finally, I look back at him.

He stubs his cigar against the lamppost and puts it in a small case he's withdrawn from a pocket. "Forsaken opportunities," he sighs.

"Excuse me?"

He backs up from the lamppost, stopping short of its funnel of light. His face is obscured by the grainy blue half-dark of a city at night. "When you look in the mirror, you regard each line or blemish with the same reluctance with which you recall a missed or discarded opportunity. It isn't too late to start finding new ones."

A loud rumble breaks the quiet behind me, and I reflexively turn around to find its source. The trolley rolls past on Central Avenue across Jackson. I turn back around and look uphill. The phantom Freud has vanished.

I continue my trek and learn from voice mail on my cell phone that my friends have decided to meet at the trendy new bar on Gay Street. I must retrace my path down the parade route to get there. I keep my sights straight ahead as I pass the alley where the graffiti critic may or may not still be lurking. Nearer the corner of Gay and Jackson, the alcove is now empty of its crying clown lady, though its blinking light bulb hangs on.

I can't help but glance in the direction of Freud's now absent apparition before wrapping my wool scarf tight around my neck and trudging onward. Several blocks south of me, the street becomes a bridge under which the Tennessee River dispatches an ice cold wind over the crest of the hill and blasting through a chute framed by Gay Street and its sundry buildings.

Standing on the north side of Summit Hill, farthest from the parade,

I idle behind acrid exhaust fumes from trucks hauling a host of gaudy floats. They bump and hiss while apple-cheeked band kids huff on their instruments. The brass of the horns and chrome of the drums gleam in the resplendent array of leafless, dormant trees, white Christmas lights coiled around their trunks and lower branches, standing in their own formation down the median of Summit Hill. Sparkling limbs outstretched, they're poised like the glittering husks of drag queens.

A whistle blows, and a luminescent red wand in the grip of an irritable-looking police officer directs me to cross the street. I march headlong into the crowd, which absorbs me, ebbs and flows like a tide as I skirt its chasing waters and dash against its eddies, cutting my own path through its foaming hordes of healthy, well-adjusted citizens of the real world. I push myself sideways against them in my maddening quest to find my party, which is down there, down a few blocks, waiting for me to arrive and open the doors for me, beckon me inside, take my coat as I stamp the dust of a long journey off my feet and sit down at last to relax.

And in between a phalanx of youth squeals in robust merriment against my charge: flag girls, tuba players, ROTCi's, majorettes, and football heroes, clustered in sequined and brocaded colors and bare flesh. And behind the vanguard, floats festooned with clowns and angels lift up the women and children first, while the old codgers in fezzes grin from the black holes of convertibles they share with beauty queens, the virgin sacrifices of any decent parade. The dizzying kaleidoscope rivets Gay Street in an endless volley of drumming, singing, tooting, humming, clanging, laughing, chanting, booming. Twirling. Dancing. Skipping. Hopping. Walking. Waving. Smiling. Falling asleep.

I hear a cheer go up and glance over my shoulder as the parade moves into its finale. There he is, Santa, fat and fake, ho ho ho-ing from his candy throne, and a mirthful clown lady stationed next to him, having touched up her makeup since her crying jag in the alcove, tosses me a strand of silver beads. Just then, as if for my eyes alone, she bends and kisses Santa. Behind this last float, that punk critic with the can of spray paint steals into a cross street.

I twirl my beads and head for my friends. Fuck age; let's live.

STIGMAS

Jessica Weintraub

Do daisies have stigmas,
she asked, like orchids?

They'd driven to a place—
 Farrington Gurney? Hinton Blewitt?
Really just a stretch of grass
along a busy road
the width of two single beds
where his favorites, *Pyramidals*, grew:
their petals a pointed cluster of ruby tears,
the color of her mouth most days.
Asphodel daisies sprouting up among them
jostled to get closer.

She caressed as many as she could,
called them "Sweetheart," "Darling."
Everything loves to be stroked
and cooed to, she explained.

He cocked his eyebrow as only an Englishman can.
That's the most American I've ever heard you sound.

She jerked her hand from the tiny fuchsia flames.
Maybe her fingertips' contour lines would transfer,
scare insects away...

At night, she searches his skin for old signs,
bites him as hard as she can, yanks
out fine hairs on his shoulders,
cuts his curls close to the skull.

She tells him she envies her friend's first love affair,
that there are no sweet ghosts to measure it against.

In fields they fall to their knees
and "make out"—a phrase he loves.
He shows her how to distinguish grasses,
whispers their Latin names into her collarbone,
one palm curved around each breast.
She loves the things he knows,
which may or may not be the same as loving him.

Besides identifying birdsong and dragonflies,
he gives her an antique key left in Abernethy Forest,
a birdfeeder he'd crafted from a silver birch log,
apologetic roses, milky tea in the mornings.
He says she never makes it hot enough.

How do bees know which species match up?
Are they aware
which of the possible powders
is sticking to them
when they next alight?

No.
But his hand grasped hers
tighter and tighter
each time they raced
across the road's blind curves.

❖

STAINED GLASS
Christopher Roethle

I was twelve when my first quiet orgasm
barbed the psalms with serifs. Twelve
when I named the befuddled hammering
mine. The stick and flush of it.
When I said—even in shame.
In the dark. There was something.
A beauty of stained glass wings
Sunday mornings in the chancel.
Aquarium blue. Cellophane yellow.
Tumbling across sacristy carpet.

Fluid. Faded angels. Found out early
I could not split these loaves and fish
against an altar. Undo cross-wired blood.
So I sang lover's oaths at midnight.
The old sacrament. The new.
Dampened sheets beneath a mounted
crucifix, sad those hymns could not tell
food from flesh. Salt from Seraphim.
True God from True God.

VICTORIA FLOATING IN POOL
Richard Remine

LAMENTATION
Ronda Redden Reitz

I am fascinated by the
  beautiful ruin of our faces,
   we women in middle age;
By the sweet slippage of our skin,
  like frosting on a cake too warm.

I am rapt by the rivulets and runlets
  that form at our brows,
By the pale blue pools
  that deepen beneath our eyes,
By the etched parentheses
  that enclose our mouths,
And make of them such dry afterthoughts.

I am enchanted by the gentle corporate merger
  taking place between our jawlines
   and our necks,
And by our necks, themselves,
  that come in three varieties—
   that I have counted thus far—
The turkey-, the turtle-, and the one
  that glides in graceful layers to our shoulders,
Like stockings 'round the ankles of
  our mother's mother's mother.

The Poet Tells of Her Orthotics

Alice Friman

My feet have met their match
in cobalt blue, stiff and unbending
as the soles of the righteous.
I have been betrayed: the whining
ligament at the bottom of each foot
has succumbed to technology
and coos in a cold cuddle of plastic.
Mold without mould, stem-cell
research in polymers: the twin
duplicates of my cocky youth
arching up to meet me. I do not like it.

But my feet, crack-brained couplet
that they are, sing in the bondage
of their shoes: *O brave new world,*
that has such cloning in't!
Poor feet. Poor little utopians
forever waiting for Prince Charming
to search them out bearing a dance card
on his cushion. How Emily's hope
flutters eternal: a Lark, a queen's
White Ibis, a Blue-footed Booby
clacking her bill and yawping on the sole.

THROUGH THE NIGHT

Linda Parsons Marion

Passing the night back and forth to the bathroom,
my belly boiling over, I normally tend the rows
of kitchen and threshold untouched by virus
or sniffle. What brought me to my knees—
the yellowfin tuna at lunch, perfectly grilled
on mesclum greens? Brush of the waiter's hand
pouring water? Throats soured as talk turned

to tears. My daughter, the stoic one, *divorce*
scalding her tongue, word she could no longer
pack like the lamps that steadied their rooms.
Did this make me retch past two—such unusual
tears neither could stomach? No easy medicine
as we journey our appointed rows, sowing
and weeding, gauging the hill country.
No dodging the roughest stones when late
at night we are humbled to the floor
by blows to the gut we never expected,
bent to our empty beginnings.

Dear Sister...
Sydney England

Reconnecting with you at this stage would be like rewiring an old Victorian mansion. It would probably take the rest of our lives if we spent every weekend at it, and I'm not sure retwining all that naked wiring would be worth it. There's truly not a lot of the girl you knew left inside here, certainly nothing resembling the silhouette on the front of your birthday card that showed up like a plane wreck in my mailbox this morning. She refused to cooperate and slept through most of what this body you see there, walking along the beach, feet just outside the frilly wave line waving sandals and squinting, has moved through. She still sleeps, one foot outside grandmother's log cabin quilt, though, dreaming Home and Garden and writing poetry no one gets.

The Girl Down the Hall

Jessie L. Janeshek

could be my daughter
if Raquelle
were sad and white. Looks like
she's always dropping acid,

and the world's
one big, bad trip.
Staring at my hair, the smell

and color of Dove soap.
Rough, uncreamy hands,
my thick, silk-coated back.
I think she'll giggle

when I sing. She almost cries.
The time we really spoke

I brought North Carolina,
sky, my pretty
piano fingers,
how I rocked Raquelle,
the swinging high

brown pines.
She was California, tall sequoias
she felt nothing under.
At the bay, light purpled

cold rainbows of haze. Gauzy air,
tang of ginger. That's the way
she told me, God-like lines

beneath her eyes, weary
and so dark I want to hold her.

DIVINER

Bill Brown

Walking across campus
near the law school
a student in a pleated skirt
and black tennis shoes
uses her white cane
to survey terrain
before her cautious steps.

My grandfather knew
a man with the gift.
He arrived one morning
with a smooth willow wand,
a dowsing rod, he called it,
to find a well in the orchard.

With the same grace
the young woman divines
the frost buckled cement,
the steps, the curb drop,
where she stops to wait
for the light to change.
She zips up her jacket
against December, straightens
the backpack on her shoulders,
speaks to an acquaintance,
laughs at a little joke,

lifts out her cane
in an even sweeping,
and crosses the busy street,
a smile lingering on her face.

My grandfather called
the diviner's gift the sight.

RIPE BLACKNESS
Christine Omodi-Engola

Here is your Blackness:
Protuberant Blackness
Proclaimed
As the Matron congratulates you,
And the OB Doc tries to date you,
And infertile couples hate you,
For the big-bellied fool that you are.
Misidentified:
The white man I ken tries to hide
Queasy loathing felt inside
When he snatches a glimpse of black hide,
Belly expanding over skin.
Guess again:
I won't be your "friend"
So you tease me, then leave me
For a yellow-haired trifle;
I'm the lonely Gwen Ifil
In a newsroom full of MacNeils.
You were wrong:
I never sang that song,
Lady Holiday blues
In a love-addict's shoes.
I kept myself clean.
Mine wasn't dirt to be seen.
It isn't a baby
In need of a daddy,

Christine Omodi-Engola

Just the Black Woman's burden
Stretching elephant skin.

Harvest

Delilah Ferne O'Haynes

I set my bucket down in loose
soil and pick off the biggest
round ripe tomato on the vine.
Time was that I would sit right
down in the dirt and bite into
that juicy red flesh, letting
the seeds ooze down my chin.
Now I put them by for winter.
Old fathers say the wise
store food for lean times.

I was saving myself for John,
the raven-haired one with the
quiet tongue and sparkling eyes.
He was smooth and warm like
sweet potato pie. I could
have devoured him in one breath,
drunk him in with one look,
and there would have been plenty
left over for a lifetime of winters.
But he wasn't the keeping variety.

The snap beans hang full
on the vine. I take them off
by the handful, feeling the solid
promise within of next year's crop

as I drop them into the bucket.
Rhythmically I work the bean row,
stopping only when I feel a chill
in the August heat, a spirit
reminder of the coming cold.
Old ones already predict frost.

Then there was Richard, with
hair like corn silk, teeth like
pearl onions in a tidy row.
He was firm and full,
like a crisp, tart green tomato,
ripe ready for my deep fryer.
But inside he was black blighted,
not worth taking off the vine.

I set my bucket down in a corn row.
One of the last ears of summer bursts
with ripeness at my touch. Remembering
the eagerness of the planting, I
tear off tender green husks,
bite into the warm juicy sweetness
of my labors. Sticky white milk drips
off my chin and oozes between my
breasts as I sit in the shade of the
corn stalks and devour the whole ear.

BODILY DRIVE

Cindy Childress

He says he should have been
a woman.
"Why can't I have one of those—
an opening wetness soft
a bouquet
of ashes pouring
from god, herself."

It's not sex he craves, but closeness.
Some transfiguration,
to crawl back inside the womb
and emerge as his partner.
An exchange of bodily parts.

Not that he wishes to be impaled,
just pillowed properly.
Not the rock, but the ocean
pulling bits of sand across a beach
where the first cell might've washed up,
and from that zygote
he would rewrite everything.

Valentine's Day: In the Supermarket

Brian Griffin

The flock of starlings
on the produce aisle

nips her neck as she bows
toward the melons

and loops her breasts
that nudge pale buds

of garlic as she bends.
Cradle of apple seed,

grape blush and ginger crotch,
secret of the kiwi's flesh:

all this is the flock's domain
and all too much for one poor bird

who breaks away and whirls
the silent whorl toward her inner ear,

touching her there like a cat's tongue
taking milk, certain only of death

and desire, oblivious of all else—
how words now fail her sheening of the air,

the luminescence of her eyes' bright hush;
how her glimmer scuffs the roses

and mocks the iridescence
of his coal-black wings.

He missed what is always
bleeding into air: the silence

of music not yet heard, the touch
of skin on skin untouched.

He missed what is beyond is,
and saw desire instead

as something holy,
something new.

BITING MY TONGUE

Debra A. Poole

At night I'm clamping, chewing,
making misery on my tongue.
In dreams I bite down
on secrets born in
innocent days,
bite down the years of dragging
his ugly baggage,
serving without pay,
the exhausted press agent.

Made brave by my own wrinkles,
I may burst at any second,
leak old wounds to brothers, husband,
the fat woman selling produce.
She has her own story to tell.
"Why do you think I eat?
With me it was an uncle."

In fantasies I spew words
grown cancerous unsaid.
An anvil flies from my chest,
fireworks launch from my head.

But my protective brain,
that Neanderthal,
senses danger,
knows the nuclear fallout of truth.
So I bite my tongue in sleep.

EXTENDED WARRANTY

Heather Wibbels

My warranty expired last month.
Dry joints grind and crack in idle,
but the sounds fade when I'm in gear.
Kidney and liver filters caked
with indigestible residue keep
my blood dark, bluish, viscous
when warm. Muscles worn thin,
microtears sealed with internal
duct tape—fascia. Bladder leaks
drip into catchalls, intermittent
dings splashing into pails. Ligaments
adhese, stuck to bones, rusty bolts
which fuse in their disintegration.

I'd like to take me back to the shop.
Lube my ligaments and joints to quiet
my stillness, solder the cracking bones
to reinforce pressure-bearing joints.
Excise blocked filters, scrub
them until light shines through.
Recondition fused muscles, replace
cracked belts, patch leaky lines and
flush the transmission to get
the old girl running smooth again.

MOM AND MISSY
Karley J. Sullivan

❊
Moving through Oz
Rebecca Efroymson

BOB DOLE'S HIGH-SPEED rail line stuttered through Carolina ridge and valley, week by week, explosion by explosion. His Viagra-brand pride shone on the television as reporters awaited the ceremonial spike outside of Asheville, North Carolina, that would connect eastbound and westbound iron. Post-trauma America anticipated a symbolic terrorist action on this stretch of tracks behind abandoned factories.

My parents and husband Bill were staying in claptrap motel rooms across the tracks from the large mansion where I was the guest of an eccentric businessman, along with several cousins. The terrorist warning signal was a series of four beeps, repeated at five-second intervals in the mansion and transmitted like Morse code to the motel, where an evacuation tunnel ran back to the basement of the mansion. There was a single evacuation that November of 2001, and everyone got out.

Images of the mansion are still clearer to me than the utilitarian features of my hospital room: the Chinese cooks and their implements, the lovely salon with curved staircase, the laundry chute mechanism in the bedroom closet, the bathtub in the middle of the living room, the chamber music and sitting rooms, the dark and sterile bedroom, and the coat closet where I kept my suitcase and plaster legs. My spare energy and remaining vocal chords were spent trying to get visitors to believe my stories. The plastic surgeon was not as used to these kinds of rants as the trauma nurses.

Bill and my mother like to remark that they are glad that my deliriums were mostly good dreams of resorts and mansions that did not reflect the horror of the auto accident and the loss of our unborn daughter. But for me there were few sugar plum fairies. My more vivid recollections include my prosthetic legs being taken out with the trash, a sociopathic woman tying me to the bed so that I would miss the evening party with my cousins, the same figure melting my glasses to my face with a small torch while onlookers did not respond to my cries, a curtainless sponge bath that was demanded and performed by the eccentric lady of the house, and my inability to get up off the floor during an aerobics class next door. I can also resurrect images of my personal health monitor interrupting an orchestra performance at the mansion and two female boaters attempting to drown me. Some of the more hopeful footage relates more closely to my true condition: that doctors from Asheville (why Asheville?) were regenerating my bones for later surgical insertion, that Bill had bought me a new house with a cadre of paid therapists in the basement, and that my daughter had been extracted from my body and was being revived and treated.

After several days post-ventilator, the mansion gradually morphed into my hospital room at a prominent regional Neurological Trauma Unit, looking more like an automobile repair bay than a bedroom. Other bays were visible across the administrative area, and the beeps of equipment behind me signaled that all was well. On second thought, a garage is not the right metaphor, because it doesn't capture the emotional range of those weeks.

I have recently taped the 1939 film *The Wizard of Oz* for my 2-year-old son to watch. The insidious contrast between the colorful munchkin dwellings and the lifeless Wicked Witch of the East, Dorothy's friendly (if odd) companions and the creepy flying monkeys, the Emerald City and the flaming projection of the Wizard of Oz recall the emotional upheaval of my subconscious at that time.

As Sam requests and watches the "Dorothy show" over and over again, it is easy to pick out a set element that is recycled in multiple scenes. A movie-screen-size window looks out onto Dorothy's Kansas farm, as well as onto the distant and encircling tornadoes and (later) a sky full of flying monkeys from the perspective of the Wicked Witch of the West. My own dreams usually began in a large landscape in and around the mansion. But they always ended on a much smaller stage through the only open curtain of my room. Sometimes, I focused on objects or events in the administrative area of the unit, such as a life-sized plaster model of vertebrae that I thought were my new bones. At other times, I was a participant in the screenplay, seated in a café where the service was slow. One evening I was terribly disappointed in the quality of the soup after waiting hours for it to come. On a particularly creative day, I constructed a building that rotated, with glass doors opening to a café, clothing store, or an aerobics studio at will. In my mind's map, these were within walking distance of the mansion.

Trauma to the head was probably not responsible for any of these visions. After 60 days of wearing an Aspen collar neck brace, we could not even see a fracture line on the original CT scan of my occipital condyle[1], at least not without the benefit of a radiologist. As the bleeding probably resulted from the collision of my hair barrette with the head rest, I no longer wear barrettes.

Nor was lack of oxygen responsible for the hallucinations. After moving me to a rehabilitation facility, a physician wrote in my chart (without the benefit of viewing CT-scan results) that it appeared that I might have "mild anoxic injury." He was troubled that I had difficulty spelling "world" backwards. On the evening of my accident four weeks earlier, I had had a severe episode of disseminated intravascular coagulation (DIC) that followed my placental abruption. In DIC, the patient's blood is unable to clot. My husband stopped counting the units of blood after 26, and my insurance was charged for 50. Nonetheless, my brain was probably never deprived of oxygen. I raced through language, math, and pattern recognition worksheets, attempting to elude dementia. The cognitive therapists teased me about being their smart patient and called upon me to help them answer questions of trivia posed by rock-and-roll radio stations. I had probably always had a backwards spelling disability, but I never had enough confidence to schedule the day-long, final diagnostic test.

It would give me some comfort to be able to identify a drug that was responsible for the vivid dreams, perhaps a sedative like Versed or Fentanyl. Then the next time my brain collides with this agent, my supporters and I will know what to expect. However, theories of cause and effect

[1]A spherical or partly spherical knob at the back of the occipital bone, which articulates with the first cervical vertebrae (the Atlas) and allows the head to sit on top of the spine.

are possible only after the effect is understood. Were my dreams more vivid than normal, or did I just remember them better? Did I dream more because I was confined to a bed? Or did my dreams pass through common themes because they were laid like tracks, one after the other, because I was sedated, and healing, and tired, and continually nodding off? We all remember our dreams more clearly when we are awakened, and as my entire family learned, a hospital is not a place for rest.

In any medical care facility one finds disruptions from blood pressure checks, medications, IV checks, monitor checks, catheter emptying, trash disposal, and meals. The purveyors of these wares do not observe traditional sleep hours, though they are less chatty at 2 a.m. than 2 p.m. To teaching hospitals is added the pitter patter of resident feet, moving like a caterpillar through the room. And in my case, visits from various specialists added to the distractions—the orthopedic surgeon (who had performed two bedside fasciotomies to relieve swelling, and to whom I owe an incomprehensible debt for retaining all of my limbs), a plastic surgeon (who unwrapped these limbs daily to rehearse future skin grafts), an obstetrician (who sampled my C-section oozes), a neurosurgeon, the trauma team, and in later weeks, various physical and cognitive therapists. However, it was an over-zealous medical resident and an enthusiastic groundskeeper who made sure that rest ceased by 5:30 a.m.

The Mexican resident spoke in three syllable phrases, always accenting the second. Good MORning. How ARE you? It's RAINing. ImPROVing. If we[2] didn't wake up when the door opened, he turned the light on and hovered over the bed, containing his enthusiasm over my improvement for a few minutes until he just had to burst. One of Bill's roles was to make assessments about which of our visitors were important to my sustenance and who could be chased away to come back some other time. He regrets that this man fooled him.

More unique, perhaps, to our location and season, was the mad leaf-blower. On the few days that we were not forcibly warmed by the sunny disposition of the resident, we were serenaded by leaf-blowers. Bill revved his complaints into the phone receiver, ending with the sidewalk

---

[2]In the first weeks, Bill was always there with me, however uncomfortable the pullout vinyl chair. Later, he took cat naps in hospital-owned hotel rooms where my parents slept.

sign that said, "please do not disturb, people are sleeping." In my dreams the engines were motorboats that visited the mansion daily. Aside from televised speeches of Donald Rumsfeld (who used many words to say nothing, over and over again), Bill's preoccupation with leaf-blowers made me smile more than anything.

As with many dreams, mine reflected aspects of reality. My rides through the bumpy laundry chute in the closet of the mansion arose from the nurses turning me over in bed to change a soiled diaper. Dreams of leg restraints were not completely fabricated. My loved ones tell me that I repeatedly tried to get out of the bed, despite injuries to my right foot, complex fractures to my left leg and arm, broken ribs, a C-section, an IV line, and a catheter. After I extubated myself while sedated, the nurses didn't want to take the chance that I might actually try to take a walk around the corridor (that lofty goal would come later).

In my dreams the sensation that I experienced most clearly was of drowning. Maintenance of a respirator requires some unpleasant plumbing. The endotracheal tube is cleared of accumulated mucus with squirts of saline solution while the patient is breathing. Then the liquid is aspirated back out with a vacuum. If one is the squirtee, then one is literally drowning for several seconds. What is less clear is how a dream (that presented complex plot with motive and opportunity) culminated in a drowning event at the same time that the tube-clearing activities occurred. Was my subconscious so aware of or conditioned by a sequence of events that always preceded the drowning? In one plot I watched my two female companions throw hazardous chemicals overboard from our boat, and when they figured out that I was going to report their activities to the authorities (and I sensed their intent to harm), we all jumped into the water. My leg was trapped on or near the boat, and one of the women pushed me under.

Myths were not confined to sleep. One falsehood that appeared in my local newspaper more than once was that my baby was delivered by helicopter paramedics while en route to the hospital. In reality, my daughter was stillborn and delivered only after her heart beat disappeared during my CT Scan. The helicopter delivery was a better story, but I never figured out who dreamed that one up. Bill's principal myth was that I would be as good as new when taken off the respirator. Instead of the articulate life companion that he knew, I was a mess; a sedated, then babbling and hoarse, and then a giddy and still hoarse mess.

The months following my automobile accident were defined by goals of a nature that were beyond my experience as a healthy, thirty-something professional. I came from a world of research, project management, and scientific communication. Though I had sometimes experienced déjà-vu from the bureaucratic themes of Dilbert comic strips, I nonetheless had convinced myself that the natural environment was a bit better off because of my scientific contributions. Also, I thought of myself as a very sympathetic and empathetic person. In contrast, healing and therapy push the patient into weeks and months of self-absorption. Goals are very limited and always have to do with self.

There were days that my goal was to take a shower and get my hair washed and other days that my goal was to avoid those hassles of taping plastic bags over open incisions and combing scabby, knotted hair. I spent hours learning how to open envelopes from well-wishers one-handed. I wanted to complete enough memory games and worksheets to pass out of cognitive therapy. Before we discovered baby wipes, I looked forward to shifts of particular nurses who wiped my bottom with a gentle hand. Weight-bearing (i.e., walking) was the holy grail that came at an orthopedic appointment when I least expected it, but before that it was a challenge just to sit up in a chair. My reward was the view of the ag-school cows on the hillside though my window[3]. Bill pointed out the cows in the same voice that he now shows our son Halloween bone-skeletons or a whole bunch of balloons or really big trucks.

I was bothered by a therapist's comment that "my affect was flat." Aside from a quick grammatical thought (isn't affect a verb?), I didn't like to think that I might never smile again or that my lack of happiness would be so evident on my face—so my goal was to act happier. Respect was also slow to come; I waited for doctors and therapists to look at me rather than my companions when discussing my progress. I never quite got used to discussions of "the arm" or "the leg" with no acknowledgment of its ownership. "Her arm" and "her leg" would have been almost as ac-

---

[3]When my condition was upgraded from critical to serious, I was moved to a room with a window.

ceptable as "your arm" and "your leg." I managed to meet everybody else's goal of getting out of the hospital for an afternoon to see the first *Harry Potter* film. But I had some anxiety about the prospect of going home, especially if in a wheelchair. Mostly, I wanted somebody to give me a date by which I would be all better.

I am glad that my character (despite the self-absorption) remained good, even in those post-ventilator days of foggy consciousness. The evidence lies in my requests for free drinks for my family (after looking around for my wallet without success). I also told my nurse that I wanted to write a book to spread hope about recovery from trauma. But months later, when I met a wheelchair-bound woman in the elevator of the rehabilitation center, whose aspect and injuries reminded me of digital photos of me, the hopeful message that I wanted to give her did not come out of my mouth. Hopefully, she saw my message in my eyes.

My lovely, stillborn daughter deserves her own story, though it will have to be fiction. Perhaps I will run some stochastic mental simulations of what she might have been and write a collection of stories with the most probable traits. What she was is not as easy to tell as what she was not.

And my friends want me to tell their story. While I was in the mansion by the tracks, they too were in a new landscape of vinyl chairs, cell phones, homeless flowers, and breaking news that was transmitted by email to a growing list of participants. But only blood relatives got to see my window into Oz.

Bodies of Forbidden Knowledge

Arthur Smith

I used to think my uncle
Harmless
Because he threatened
To burn down
His house for
The insurance money.
He wasn't even my uncle,
But my father's cousin.
So when he did, it was
Hard to believe.
Arson, he sneered.
It was like listening
To Butch Carroll
Boasting in the over-
Heated cafeteria
Of feeling up what's
Her name's *cunt*. It was
The first time I ever
Heard that word, such
Full-throated urgency
In the way he owned it,
The way he turned
It in his hand
In the air.

❈
ANOSMIA
Jo Ann Pantanizopoulos

Aroma, fragrance, essence, redolence, stench, odor, stink.
All gone.
I sit and breathe in remembering
Heavy garlic tomato sauces bubbling on my stove,
Licoricey ouzo and salty feta,
My children's necks even now and
Thinking of their womb wet perfume at birth.
I pass by the basil bush on Mamá Vera's veranda
Awakening the heady mist of nose-pleasure brushed by
my skirt's hem.
I breathe again bringing in burned toast, dirty diapers, and
My mother's Mexican cornbread with hot chiles
and melty cheese.
I watch from my swing amidst the swirling attar of
crushed jasmine
As my little ones squeal and press the fallen white flowers
with their bare feet.

Somewhere on the Aegean, somewhere between
Mykonos and Patmos,
A smell-robbing virus, the Greek god of a hacking cough,
met my wet bathing suit
And attacked my olfactory epithelium blocking
those neurons from
Sending fried onion molecules to my brain.

Without *osmi*, without my sense of smell.
I can go live with the skunks now
And pass by rotting garbage and pass up Clinique's Aromatic
Elixir on sale.
I'll decline the taste test of "Too much salt?" and
"Add more lemon?"
Pouring out last month's jug of milk in the fridge
doesn't bother me.
I'll be happy to wipe the baby's bottom and walk over
fetid road-kill
And wait for the feast of boiled cabbage to invite me back.

I'll eat and smell and dream now by working on memory,
Sucking on a clove, hoping someday, to return to my
mother's pumpkin pie.

A FLUTTER (PRAISE DANCE)

Alicia Benjamin-Samuels

First, a flutter.
Then I felt her shake and roll.
She shimmied—
vibrated her house,
my womb,
better than Billie Holiday's vibrato.
She quivered and wiggled like she was at her first
camp meeting—
like she already knew how to praise and shout
with her sweet birch,
willowy body.
Giovanni Gicina was a dancer in my dreams
before she was born.

THE SCENT OF PRAIRIE AIR

Rebekah Goemaat

The sweet odor of curious poison
Blows on this prairie air.
Poison that slows the diaphragm
Thickens the tongue
That presses fluid around each joint
Impeding motion,
Like the padding small children
Wear to play football.

This scent smells of the unreal
Of my parents curious point of view
The eternal fundamentalist optimists,
Joyfully approaching judgment.
On the kitchen wall, the bird clock chirps
"Life is simple."
While the black clock behind the piano ticks
"All is well."

Liars! Beneath this façade
This joyful ticking off the time
My mother's heart has ceased
To beat in even rhythm
My father's bones grow stiff
And ache with age and over-work.

My parents' house, foundation first,

Sinks slowly into the Iowa earth
With no one to raise it.
My father's arms are too feeble,
The eye of my mother's mind too clouded
To see her slanting kitchen floor.

The walls of this house bend their backs
A little more each year, acquiescing
To the irrational demands of the floor
Eighty-year-old electric wires touch dry timbers
As these walls with no smoke alarms
Wait for a spark to set them free.

Damn the clocks that hang on these walls,
Chirping their lies,
Ticking away the time in this forsaken landscape!
Where all is decay, where all around
Old houses, old barns, old bones fall down
With no care.

And without care
My parents' walls too will fall
Without beta blockers
My mother's arrhythmic heart will fail.
One day, my father's old bones
Will stand still.

And where my parents once lived
In this place where I was born
Birds will light on the trees
My dead grandfather planted
Chirping away their songs,
While all around them, night and day
Prairie grasses blow.

Earth's Daughter

Donna Doyle

Earth called me early.
Gentle slope of red clay dirt
offered handfuls, poured
over my skin,
rubbed in hard until
I could see no difference
between pale flesh and dark soil.
Not burial, but revival,
source calling out to source
in a language I am still deciphering.
Medium to planet spirit,
I laugh.
I cry.
The sound echoes back in time
toward dirt now covered with tangled ivy,
somewhere underneath
the outline of a small girl
stretched out, patiently waiting to be
recognized as earth.

WHAT IS LEFT?

Andrew Najberg

My mother's nipples must sag off
the sag of her breasts like the leaf
crown of a strawberry too long
on the vine and her fiancé sucks
them voraciously with the fervor
of his twenty two year junior
after nights drinking. She could
legally drink before he was born,
hopping blues bars in New York
off from a ten hour day learning
binary to run the bank computers
back when her ankles were slender
as sideways silhouettes on stilettos.

I am sure it terrifies her during sex
that her stamina is not sixty New York
minutes and ticking. Bed springs creak
different when body is a fight. Couched
back on red recliner, our B-horror double
feature Monday, her head dips and snaps
back. With a stubbed cigarette and empty
cup, she slips into a snoring sleep before
we even glimpse the monster, and I watch
her frown in her soundness. Soundless,
I know that one day, she will die.

And I must admit that it's hard to reconcile
my mother's new lover. Loneliness, I thought,
when they met when I wasn't there for her,
wrapped up in my own romantic wranglings.
One night, I dropped by her apartment
to find him naked on her couch quick enough
to cover up but too tongue tangled with
Tennessee whiskey to introduce himself.
I remember her blush when she slunk
through the bedroom door in her bathrobe,
the v of the fabric cross dipping down
to her freckled chest. I felt violated
as I visualized work-rough, redneck palms
pressing the points that gave me suck.

Part of me would have loved
it if she became a nun, but
what does she do for a living?
Nurses. Down at Ashbury
Place, sixteen-hour double
shifts, tends the fading lights
of the terminals. Unlike
the other nurses who shuffle
about in their white shoes
with soft soles, my mother
understands the real nature
of binary. No zeros and ones.
Only signal and no signal.
Alive and not alive.

Two in the morning, I shuffle coat
sleeves and bootlaces in the dim lit
living room before I wake her
by shaking her stockinged foot.
She snorts, looks left, right as if

to make sure no one's listening
and asks why I didn't wake her.
I tell her she needs her sleep,
works at seven, but really
I remember the day she told me
her left lung partially collapsed.

At my own bedroom window
for sunrise, the view covers
an empty stream bed between
apartment buildings. The gaggle
of white rocks tilt jagged edges
to keep each other crooked.
A little bridge with rusted rails
because there is no proper footing
in mutual support. As I gaze
across the grass that glistens
in the ascending sun with memories
of the stars, I also stand in the center
of the span. Winter storms wore
down its point of anchor. I rock
cradled in the wind, pulverized.
A possum licks inside a broken
eggshell under the tree where
I found a half-eaten fledgling.

UNTITLED
Karley J. Sullivan

The Soul of Hands

Joe Rector

THE FAMILY SHARED a celebration lunch after my daughter's college graduation. Midway through our entrée, one of my nieces came to me at the end of the meal to tell me that my daughter's future father-in-law reminded her too much of Dal, my older brother who died in January. Vanessa whimpered, "What bothered me so much is Mr. Chemsak's hands look so much like Dal's."

I peered up from my plate and saw that, in fact, the man's hands had the same shape as my brother's. The ache inside my own heart rushed forward as I realized that hands tell much about a person. They are every bit as much "windows to the soul" as our eyes.

A person's hands cannot lie. They tell about the work the individual performs. The calluses and skin like tanned leather show a man who has spent much of his time in manual labor of some kind. The softness of a woman's hand indicates her dedicated attention to her skin and its silkiness. I remember when I met Billy McCool, a relief pitcher for the Cincinnati Reds in the mid 60s. When I shook his hand after a ball game, a chill ran through me for I had never shaken a man's hand that was so smooth and soft and well-manicured. Of course, generalizations don't apply to hands because many women have rough hands from working in demanding careers, and some men have soft hands due to the ease their jobs afford.

For many, hands are part of communication. Just as a person needs his tongue, lips, voice box, and other anatomical parts to speak, his hands become vital parts of his speech; those extremities help to give our conversations feelings, emotions, senses of urgency, and absoluteness to our convictions. In fact, some individuals truly are "tongue-tied" without their hands. Even the shapes that hands make help to convey our messages. A fist indicates anger; a pointed finger alerts others that a parental lecture is being administered; hands raised in the air with palms turned toward the sky indicate that a person is at a loss for an answer to a problem.

Hands convey our emotions much better than our mouths. When someone close is hurting, the best means of showing love, support, and understanding is hug accompanied by a pat. Just a gentle rubbing of the back is calming and assuring to the most upset person. Quick blows to another's body show either playfulness of teenaged boys or anger of another for some serious offense that has been committed. Adults remember the swift swats to the bottom when they crossed the line and faced one of countless childhood punishments. The justice administered by those guiding hands stopped temporarily youngsters' run-ins with parental law.

The loved ones lost over the years are many times remembered by their hands. My dad died when I was thirteen, but what I most vividly recall about his lifeless body in that coffin are his hands. They were covered with dark hair on the backs, and most often they were posed at the kitchen table. One curled around a faded green coffee cup, and the other pressed against his forehead. Between the first two fingers was a Winston with its smoke curling upward and filling the room with its haze. Those hands had prepared a feast at Christmas time as my father spent a sleepless Christmas Eve hourly basting the turkey for the next day's meal. As he lay there, his hands had forever lost their ability to perform those loving tasks for family.

The thing I found most difficult to comprehend on the death of my father-in-law was the stillness of his hands. Vaden Netherton had, for years, made barn wood frames and other pieces of furniture. His hands were wide and strong. In the evenings he watched television and whittled green pieces of willow, which he used to construct primitive tables. On fingers, knuckles, and palms were any number of scars from mishaps with knives or slipping tools used on natural gas lines he installed and repaired. I couldn't imagine those hands unable to create those things. How could the hands of this craftsman be stilled so quickly?

My mother was a woman slight in stature. She stood a mere five feet, two inches. Her zest for life made up for lack of height. She often talked about how her own mother's hands were so ugly. Yet, her hands became replicas of the ones she found so unappealing. Bony fingers gave them a gnarled appearance; however, mother's crooked index fingers possessed magical powers. With them she poked holes into the rich soil, and there plants were guaranteed to grow. Those same hands prepared suppers for three constantly hungry boys and any other stray friends we dragged through the front door.

Most agonizingly, I remember my older brother's hands. They weren't big, but they had worked long enough to enable him to play the guitar quite well. His hands could also write some letters that, when I was a teenager, preached hellfire and brimstone. Those hands never touched us as fists, but the words penned by an older brother forced to become a surrogate father set my feet on the straight and narrow for a while.

I often think of the hands of my family. My daughter's hands seemed so tiny. I held them tightly as if I needed the safety of her grip more than she needed mine. I can recall Dallas's hands as he put on that first baseball glove, and we went outside to play ball for a while. The games of catch were for me, not for him. Most of all, I still remember the time I held my wife's hand on our first date. It was an awkward moment, but when I did take her hand, it seemed to fit perfectly. After all of these years of marriage and children and jobs and fussing and fighting, her hand is the only one that always fits the same as it did back then.

I am a lucky guy who has been blessed with loving people. My hope is that when it is my time to pass that someone will think of my hands with good memories and will remember their worthwhile accomplishments.

13 1/2

Christine Parkhurst

It's the strangest thing

The older I get

The more frizzy-haired

And

Big

The more gorgeous sexy

Brilliant moody totally-awesome

Clever and

Challenging

Becomes my daughter

[liaison with a lullaby]

Natalia Nazarewicz

i almost cannot believe that
someone could be so at ease

two fingers reposed on your cheek as your
ribcage moves rhythmically

your velvet neck like a bird's wing
reaches towards
complementary coral lips
barely parted, like threads in unraveling string
enclosing tacit thoughts
and fragile willow whispers
products of your trance,
the willful hypnosis you undergo daily

i glance over to listen to
the almost-laboured breathing
short bursts of
revitalization
alternate with
purifying mellowness,
release,
satisfaction,
inhale!
seize and let go.

my journey east stops
as i try to discern
if embossed half-spheres
track my own eyes' movements
from behind their closed shutters
(they look upwards instead)

i dare not ask what you dream of
and you dare not tell—

upon awakening, you will have forgotten
upon asking, you would never return
schrödinger's cat trapped in pandora's box
who longs to forget her secrets

(but they're sacred anyway)

THE YOUTH

Margery Weber Bensey

She wanted to feel his cheek against hers.
It would be smooth, because he was young,
he was young and unruined
and she wanted his joy.
She wanted to touch him, she wanted
to feel how smooth he would feel
his face and his unruined body
but she was afraid to touch him, not
because she would frighten him
like some shy bird he would flee her
but because she knew if she came
close enough, she would find that
his life was not unruined, his body
was not smooth, and that
he would look at her and tell her
that there is no joy.

*

Interlude:
Reading Virginia Woolf
Pam Strickland

My body is the place where I take possession of my world; it firmly attaches me to a kingdom of things, it ensures that I will have a solid base in the world, a station, a remaining in it, a dwelling in it.
~Bruce Callieri

OBSESSED.

This was my professor's conclusion when my only comment about Theresa of Avilla was that she was considered one of history's first identifiable anorexics. It had only been a week or two since her likeness had graced the cover of the staid *Journal of the American Medical Association*.

My classmates preferred disbelief and disinterest. The course is History of the Essay, a 7000-level reading seminar. The woman, who initiated discussion of writing by the 13th century mystic, quickly dismissed me as a bit touched. A not uncommon reaction to my ramblings about the way women look at the physical container of their soul in this world where they are objectified instead of treasured, respected. By refusing acknowledgement of my comment, Theresa's fan indicated that disordered eating had nothing to do with this saint's crystalline musings. Never mind that the JAMA article had implied that religiously-inspired fasting frequently had been for reasons other than spiritual insight.

Shortly after, he joined my fellow students in their dismissive state; however, in an aside my professor whispered that my obsession was a good sign that my research into how a teacher's body image affects student-teacher interaction in the composition classroom was eking into every aspect of my studies, my life. Nonetheless, my classmates, all at least two semesters away from the thesis process, clearly wanted no more knowledge.

So, when a reading of Virginia Woolf's ethereally beautiful "Street Hauntings: A London Adventure" left me considering other body images, other ways of linking the self and the body, I decided not to speak, instead absorbing her words:

> "The shell-like covering which our souls have excreted to house themselves, to make for themselves a shape distinct from others is broken, and there is left of all these wrinkles and roughnesses, a central oyster of perceptiveness, an enormous eye."

The tough fragility of a shell covering: What would there be of me were there no covering? What would my wrinkled, torn soul do? Where would it rest?

Then the professor mentioned Woolf's much debated manic-depression, which reportedly led her to put rocks in her pockets and walk into the River Thames and drown. My confession was that, although I had never read much Woolf, I had come across a number of references to her childhood sexual abuse, so it was difficult for me to read anything about or by her without thinking, "This is an incest survivor." Then I silently added, "like myself." Nor did I speak aloud of the exceedingly high commorbidity of eating disorders and depression in incest survivors.

My classmates exploded, everyone talking about the supposed mental state of the famous and prolific English writer whose image seemed everywhere in our community of university professors and grad students. Instead of dissecting Woolf's essay, they were debating her mental state and family life, just how much of her writing directly connected to that muddled mind. I remained quiet about the body stuff. Later, when the evening's discussion turned to our only writing assignment for the course—a critical essay on some aspect of the essay—I was glad for my reticence. The very words, "rhetoric of the body" regarding my desire to keep my paper in the same area as my thesis research lead to an interrogation that surely rivaled that of Monica Lewinsky at the hands of Kenneth Starr's staff.

"What do you mean?"

"How can the body communicate?"

I told them of Judith Butler's *Bodies that Matter*, Susan Bordo's *Unbearable Weight*, Elizabeth Grosz's *Volatile Bodies*. They stared the stare of cluelessness. They did not know of the wild French women—Irigaray, Cixous, Kristeva—who talk of our bodies as being essential to who and what we are.

The works of Michel de Montaigne, the Frenchman who initiated writing of essays, were suggested for my seminar paper. To me, Montaigne's bottom line was always acceptance of what is. Yet, I could not relate his carrying-ons about his liver with my own self-consciousness in relating to people of normal size. Put bluntly, the man bored me.

Every topic that sparked the least bit of interest in my weary soul turned out to be extended nonfiction, not a contained essay. Days later, my professor listened as I offered *Wasted*, a work by an anorexic with intellectual leanings. He shuffled the papers and books on his desk, shaking his head, beginning to speak, then refraining. Finally, in a subdued mumble he said he'd try to look it over. He was questioning me too. Could no one see my truth? Could no one feel my truth? The truth I knew at every level from the reflection in the mirror to the very core of my soul.

Despite its repeated appearance in my research, I had tried hard to avoid *Wasted*, only giving in after hearing an NPR interview with the author. I probably would have stuffed it back on the shelf at the local Barnes & Noble if not for the epigraphs and the Works Cited list, which included rhetoricians such as Michel Foucault, as well as Butler and Bordo. Plus, the author's writing was at a level beyond what usually shows up in memoirs of starving and purging.

In the meantime, a friend was busy searching out a topic for her own term paper. Her professor, the department chair, had rather succinctly told me earlier that my compulsive appearance concerns had nothing to do with my teaching. He went so far as to compare me with T.S. Eliot's lamenting J. Alfred. After observing my classroom performance, he said my students were not relating to my size, but were instead relating to my respect for them and my expectations of them. Still, I listened as this friend, who also fights disordered eating, told me she had come across a web site where the author had contended that by today's standards, Woolf was considered not only manic-depressive but also anorexic. I was tired of disordered eating being such a constant in the work on body image, but it seemed the only way to get to what I wanted to discuss.

Then came a book my thesis chair owned but had never read, *All that Summer She was Mad: Virginia Woolf and Her Doctors* by Stephen Trombley. I began reading. On page five there is mention of Woolf's periodic refusals to eat. Page ten brought the first mention of anorexia accompanied by Trombley's conclusion regarding Woolf's supposed madness: "It does seem to me, however, that there is a means by which one central factor of all Virginia's breakdowns and illnesses can be profitably illuminated. I refer to a phenomenological analysis at the level of the body: an analysis of embodiment." He explains:

> "During all of Virgnia's breakdowns, she had a peculiar relationship to her body. She felt that it was sordid; she found eating repulsive; she felt as if her body was not the centre of her 'self'—that she somehow existed at odds with it, or divorced from it. Not only is a problematical sense of embodiment a central factor in all of her breakdowns, but it is also one of the perennial themes of her novels and, indeed, of her essays, letters and diary."

For the first time in months, I was not only obsessed but invigorated. The body, not just any body, but the body of the much-loved, admired, and read Virginia Woolf was a body tortured much the same as mine, only the opposite. Her body shriveled as she refused to eat, so malnourished that she frequently went months without a menstrual cycle. My body exploding like a slightly heated marshmallow, in such an estrogen overload that it repeatedly overproduces uterine nourishment in a way that leads to excess menstrual-like bleeding. Women at each end of the century, on either end of the eating disorder compendium, each wanting to bear a child but unable for various reasons, probably connected to misuse of her own childhood, to do so. Each woman trying desperately to write her way out of the insanity of it all while abusing her body and confounding the medical professionals with depressive, destructive episodes just outside the realm of reality.

Most of the references in the Trombley book connecting the work and the woman concerns Woolf's fiction. Initially, the only essays by her that bore up to my scrutiny for embodiment references were the ones in our course textbook, "Street Hauntings: A London Adventure" and "The Death of the Moth." Yet we had been instructed to go beyond the works in our anthologized text in our research. I whined silently, thinking of how "Moth" so carefully, gently describes the ceasing of function in the body of this creature while looking only momentarily at the state of its soul.

Putting it aside, I began a campaign to read as much Virginia Woolf as possible in the month or so remaining in the semester. During the same time I read more and more of Butler and Bordo and even Mikhail Bakhtin as part of my thesis-obsessed state. Plus, I taught Comp II for the first time. This seems insane. Why couldn't I acknowledge that the discussion, the detailed deconstruction of essays we had discussed in class had impacted my writing and my teaching? That should be enough to get a grade in the course. It seemed there had been times I had been given a grade for less. But no, I was on a campaign to become an instant expert on Woolf.

Had this not always been my way? An all or nothingness to life. I would be a student; I would be a reporter. I could not be both. I would be a writer; I would be a reader. But not both. I would be a student, a teacher, but never the two equally. One role always suffered. I would eat balanced healthy meals, exercise, and get enough sleep. But, no, if I did that I could not concentrate on being any of the other things that I was committed to because I would feel much too much of the pain of life. So, I must eat, compulsively and secretly because if I did it in the open, they would know that I was trying to snuff my very life out, much as Woolf tried and tried all those years. If she could control her fleshly desires, she would not have to be punished for being a bad girl. If she could numb herself through starvation then she could forget the pain of having been treated as less than human, as a person without feelings, without desires, without respect and individuation.

I started reading *Orlando* again, a project taken on as examination of the role the gendered body we are given at birth and how adorning that body affects identity. Remembering the course was the History of the Essay, not the History of the Novel, I put the book aside in favor of *A Room of One's Own*, where Woolf takes a stand for feminist writers; then *Moments of Being*, Woolf's journal entries published posthumously as essay-like material. Finally, I turned to the book loaned me by my professor, *The Death of the Moth and other Essays*.

Forgetting that *Moth* was in our class reading, I tackle it again. There is Woolf contemplating the moth:

> "One is apt to forget all about life, seeing it humped and bossed and garnished and cumbered so that it has to move with the greatest circumspection and dignity. Again, the thought of all that life might have been had he been born in any other shape caused one to view his simple activities with a kind of pity."

What if that life, that life of Virginia had been born inside another shape, a shape that penetrated instead of received, a shape that inherited wealth and headed families instead of being married off and being headed by others? Would she have been taken advantage of? Would she have been instructed sexually against her will, or would she have been expected to do that sexual instruction?

I reread the page. A paragraph earlier contains the sentence—"What he could do he did"—paraphrased but nonetheless the very sentence I had heard when dealing with my own disordered life. I had been angry with myself for all the missteps taken. Angry at family members I thought could have protected me. Angry at God on general principles. Repeatedly, cutting through the anger was the voice of reason, the voice of healing: "I/You/They did the best I/you/they could at the time."

Sure.

Is that not what Woolf did? She could not take away the pain and embarrassment of the fondling by her half-brother. She could not remove the trepidation of the emotional death that came when the mania waned. She could not throw off the heaviness of the depression. Incest was not spoken of openly then. The impact not fully understood by either society or the medical profession. Depression was spoken of in whispers and treatment debated heavily by the leaders in the fledging psychiatric field, a fact that is reinforced by the exploration in Trombley's book. Anorexia was heard of, but barely. It was not seen as a means of control, but as a means of insanity. Perhaps it still is. Like the moth, Woolf did what she could; she starved the pain away. Starved the agony away. When that did not work, she also did as the moth: "The moth having righted himself now lay most decently and uncomplainingly composed. O yes, He seemed to say, death is stronger than I am." She might have added, stronger than the voices in my head, the anguish in my soul, the pain of this earthly body.

Then I remember this essay is excluded from the writing assignment and I cry, but only metaphorically.

I find copies of *Common Reader*, both volumes, in the library and I am overwhelmed by their thickness, intimidated by the yellowing of the pages. The books get put aside. I purchase copies of *Three Guineas*, *Woman and Writing*, and a book of literary criticism entitled *Virginia Woolf and the Real World*. I am overwhelmed by the quantity and quality of the works. I am overwhelmed by the nuances in all those words. I am overwhelmed by the very fact that I have attempted to undertake such research in the midst of this stressful time of my life.

Late one night when I should be writing, instead of thinking, I find myself reading. I had not been impressed by the critical essays written by Woolf we read for class, but I am a woman of desperation. My eyes end up on an essay in the *Moth* book about the work of George Moore, Woolf's contemporary:

"But are not all novels about the writer's self, we might ask? It is only as he sees people that we can see them; his fortunes colours and his oddities shape his vision until what we see is not the thing itself, but the thing seen and the seer inextricably mixed."

Suddenly, I am clairvoyant. It is only a couple of days since I returned to a sane eating plan, a healthy approach to the way I deal with my body so that I can deal with life on life's terms, instead of numbing the pain of my reality. I had spent the last few weeks, no, the last few months, eating everything I could find with the same determination that Leonard Woolf described in his dairies that his wife had approached not eating. I am in the midst of my own insanity. I realize with a clarity not previously possessed that Woolf's words ring true for me because I know that whatever I write reflects my state of mind, my sanity. Just as she knew 50 years ago that all those words she wrote, all the observations she had, would paint a picture of her sanity, her reality, for the world to explore and that no matter how hard she might try that it all came down to the way she felt about herself, her soul, and its container.

❊

ARRHYTHMIA

Jane Sasser

In humans, the size of the heart
is the size of the fist.

Six weeks after your birth,
an event which had seemed
so commonplace,
I watched the blurs on the ultrasound,
the swirls and whooshes
pinpointing the hole
inside your beating heart.
Betrayed by this failure of odds,
I nodded at the doctor's words,
ears ringing with pounding blood.
Riding home through
a budding spring,
the landscape hemorrhaging
vibrant green,
I thought of the months to come,
how hourly I'd watch your face
for tinges of blue,
hold my breath to hear your sigh,
feel your chilled fingers wrap
around my own like locks,
and know you needed no fist
to inflict this pain.

MORNING

Sylvia Woods

Gray dawn filters
through gauzy curtains,
flutters on the ceiling,
amorphous as moths.

 From the kitchen come thuds,
of Mommy's feet as she pads from stove
 to counter, humming
 "I'm just going over Jordan,"
Just going... over home."

Outside birds twitter in trees.
while I snuggle in warm quilts,
close to sister, her breath a whisper.

Mommy's shoes swish as she moves,
sifting flour, kneading biscuits.
The coffee pot perks, blur-blurb,
wafting fragrance like a morning kiss.
In that even stillness another sizzle,
sausage in the iron skillet.

Then, while the house sleeps,
she whispers, "Frank"
and bedsprings creak twice
as he rolls over once,

turns again, sighs hard,
slams both feet on the floor
a decisive thud.

Then a yawing stretch,
the whoosh of boots over socks,
boot strings' scream, and then
sturdy tread crosses wood and linoleum,
straight to the steaming food

where the scrape of the chair precedes
clatter of fork on plate,
slam of screen door as he
leaves for work that will sustain.

So Little Remains

Frank Jamison

So little remains of what I was,
The scattered pieces tossed into corners,
An old room with a broken box,
Blocks of alphabet beside the stove,
Some war souvenirs in the garage.

If I can recall the pieces, I can
Rebuild myself, but then what shall I do
With these fragments of what I've become,
This slick armor, this strange place.
Where shall I put them all?

The distant hills try to tell me what I am
And was and will become;
The night hawk and night heron
Speak to me in the same language;
The river sighs like my mother.

These things I have gathered
Are not what I am, though I am
Part and parcel of them all
Like a sea shell containing
The few remains of what it was.

�֎

BARBIE GOES GRAY

Judy Lee Green

"BARBIE GOES GRAY" was the headline of a recent Mattel press announcement, accompanied by a very unflattering picture of the teenage icon in an evening gown. She was wearing large retro, pink-rimmed eyeglasses and sporting a brand new granny-do in steel-wool gray.

Barbara Millicent Roberts burst upon the American scene in 1959 as a sixteen-year-old fashion model. Do the math. If she was sixteen in 1959, Barbie is now sixty-two years old! Slim, trim, trendy yet stylish, she still wears form-fitting Spandex, teensy-weensy bikinis and stiletto heels. The only clue that she has joined the ranks of senior citizens is her Brillo Pad gray hair.

Frankly I am amazed that she ever cut her long blonde locks and let her hair go gray. Why would she? Is she about to come out of the closet and admit to age-defying secrets or plastic surgery, perhaps breast augmentation? Look at her! Her boobs stand at attention straighter than a new recruit at Ft. Jackson, South Carolina. At sixty-two, and without surgery, her nipples should be pointing to South America, not Ontario, Canada! If she were truthful, she would admit to having one hell of a backache, carrying around breasts the size of two canned hams.

Barbie's thighs are as slim and sculpted as those of a six-year-old girl. Of course, she's bound to have had liposuction. Perhaps the fat from her thighs was injected into her breasts. Her unlined face is not the face of a sixty-two year old woman. No doubt she has had Botox and collagen injections, chemical peels, and microdermabrasion on a regular basis. Otherwise, her face would not look like a newborn baby's butt.

Mattel should encourage Barbie to be honest and frank and share with her sisters how she has avoided the pitfalls of aging. Why, after years of cramming her size eight feet into size five stiletto heels, does she not have corns, heel spurs, or hammertoes? It's obvious that she has had varicose veins stripped from her legs or they would not be as smooth as a department store dummy's. As a sun worshipper and a yacht owner, how has she avoided dry itchy skin, the heartbreak of psoriasis or even skin cancer?

I can't begin to imagine the distress she has endured while maintaining a dazzling white, beauty pageant, capped-tooth smile while suffering from constipation. And don't tell me the bitch does not have it, because if she's sixty-two, she's on half-a-dozen different medications that cause irregularity.

Is it true or only a rumor that Mattel insisted on Barbie going gray, with not even a blue rinse for her hair, to prepare collectors for the release of the Christmas collection in the fall? Are they really coming out with a Red Hat Barbie in droopy socks, comfortable shoes, mismatched skirt and blouse, and an oversized purple sweater? Will she really be holding a Beech-Nut Baby Food jar with six gallstones in it?

I understand that Barbie's sixty-two year old best friends will be available for the holidays also. How nice. Perhaps their mouths will move and they will talk about their hysterectomies. What fun. Bounce them up and down and simulated light urine leakage will appear on their pantiliners. Any woman who once loved a Betsy-Wetsy will delight in owning one of these lifelike aging supermodels.

If Barbie expects to have any friends in her old age, she should level with us women. How has she managed to avoid, at the age of sixty-two, a back seat as wide as a '73 Buick? What about PMS and chocolate? What about bread? What about hamburgers and French fries and milk shakes? I admit that Barbie looks great, but how has she maintained her sixteen-year-old, 39" by 23" by 33" measurements? She couldn't have worked out very much. She has walked on her tippy-toes for the last forty-six years.

I have been a fitness enthusiast for many years, but my body does not look like hers. I wonder how often Barbie checks her weight. I weigh myself almost every day so that extra pounds do not creep up on me. I remove my shoes, take off my clothes, spit out my gum, pop out my contacts, take off my earrings, blow my nose, clear my throat and spit before I weigh, but I never lose a pound. Barbie, tell us your secret, please!

With boats and cars, a jet plane, a motor home, closets full of clothes, and many successful careers, it seems that Barbie has had it all. Does she regret not marrying Ken and settling down and having a house full of kids? Rumor says that she and Ken have broken up. Apparently it was Cali, the sweet young California girl recently hired by Mattel, who came between them.

Ken is reported to have said that he liked steamy hot young Barbie, but didn't like sweaty old Barbie with hot flashes. Well, good riddance to him. I understand that Mattel is coming out in a couple of years with early Alzheimer Ken complete with bedpan, walker and other nursing home accessories.

If Mattel plans a retirement Barbie in three more years when she reaches the age of sixty-five, I hope that she has a big rear-end with a wide-load sign on it, drooping breasts (size 39 long), fallen arches, thinning hair, liver spots, and trifocals. She should complain about sore, stiff aching joints, brittle bones, fatigue, and memory lapses.

She should have teeth in a jar, a hearing aid, a dark mustache, and must be wearing a housecoat and scruffy slippers. Her bladder should drop like a yo-yo when she sneezes. Little girls will scream and flee from her, but she'll sell, to all the women who have been expected to look like a Barbie doll for the last forty-six years. She'll sell.

SILICON
Bradford Tice

I

With day's slow heat, we return to the bar
where we met. You drink Crown, while I slug back
jewelers' hammers. Over rum shots, I tell
you I'm leaving for school in fall. You say,
let's drink to love. Earlier, Michael called
for a chauffeur to the Silicon Ball.
Not knowing what he meant, I agreed.
Already, bulbs of breasts, like chanterelles, peek through
his shirt. You scoff into your drink, amber-
light, heady fumes. The smell of ambergris
wafts from your wrist. You say, *even gay men*
should act like men, then grab your cock and pull—
a gesture I find entrancing, cheeky.
Pressed beneath these sheets of days, I give in.

2

Dream a siege of birds of paradise, you'd
come close—spears of feathers gored in claret,
tears of lapis. In the motel, drag queens
arrange themselves on chairs, sit Indian-
style on the cusps of beds. Driving over
in the car, Michael tells me he'll soon be
a woman. Waiting in cool of the room,
circled by shows of royalty, I think
of you. Before leaving, you asked if we'd

weathered the storm. I never answered.
Masks grin from all sides. An ever growing
absence patterns the windows—burns of frost.
Deception is an honest show at living—
ask any queens in ersatz tiaras.

3

After four rounds of shots, you slur words.
Say things like, *We'll keep in touch, love can dare
distance.* I say, *We should see other people.*
Two years will feel a lifetime. Through smoke,
vivid globes ricochet across felt lawns.
A man, in a second-skin of jeans, chalks
his stick. Stacks of quarters glow like moons.
You motion, *we could take him home, just to see.*
I catch what's meant, but before I say, *yes,*
something gives within me. Outside, trees drop
color. Our table a wreck—glass and swill.
You skin labels off bottles of beer, slit them
to tatters, then arrange them on the bar
like a conundrum. You point and summon.

4

These are not social creatures. Yet they come
with their needs etched in hard lines of jaws.
Light grips the tight architecture of cheeks.
They wait, bejeweled hands held placid in pools
of their laps, cake of make-up hardening.
Mistress Sable arrives. I watch as she takes
from her bag a syringe, clear bottles
of silicon. For hard cash she injects
cheeks, hips and lips, anywhere you covet—
fill out taut until curves manifest.
What's wanted is ability to change.
Come one, come all, Sable says. *I have my*

anodynes and potions, buoyancy in carafes.
Sable knows, sugar, light can be so harsh.

5

He struts to our table—ivory bull,
ivory swan. Grace and belligerence.
His name is Paul. You throw on charm, a red
garland. We present ourselves, give false names.
Through the impossible white of his shirt,
nipples like buttons insinuate.
It's hard, this tendency toward the new, never
been tasted. Something was mislaid here.
Already, this loss like an amputee's itch,
junkies for a needed solace—a fleeting
fix. You look to me for direction.
I blow kisses as we three exit the door.
Outside, solid weather, west wind whistles
right through us. Hollow echo, hallowed horn.

6

Michael grips my fist as needle goes in.
Pants around his knees, his prick like a pulled-
up root, Michael winces as gleaned earth
adheres to his thigh. Sable titters at his
cringe, swats at the tuber distended
between his legs. *Shame to split somethin' so*
ripe. Michael beams. Before arriving, we
gossiped about Sable's past. How she was
barred from the bright stages of Atlanta
for sneaking crushed glass into the compacts
of her competition. *She's had a rough life.*
Like me, Michael says. His shadow lengthens,
hips swell to birthing. He's stillborn—still
changing. Scrotum pulls up, tucks itself inside.

7

How should I speak of raw desire? Let's say,
underneath the skin of denim, wolf-scent.
Pores pressed lip-to-lip form wet chambers, cells.
Out of blue, this trinity and too much
sensation. Bristles of your face are flecks
of lodestone, while novel calluses press
the small of backs. Three threads make intricate
knots. Then, startling climax—veins fired
in the eyes like flares, burning syringes.
After, fading idols exit at the door,
and then alone with you. In my mind is
a crawl space barely four feet wide. Something
inside decides to fail, to come undone.
I need an image. A clean show of faith.

8

I met Michael working at a subs shop.
He was what we called, *obvious. Hopeless.*
First night, he told me he was a woman
trapped in the case of man. Later, closing,
he confides that at thirteen, his mother
sold him to a carny for the price
of a fix. *She was a junkie from way back.*
The carny ran a lemonade stand for
roving fairs. Days, Michael squeezed bitterness
into cups. At night, the carny groped him
in the dark, smell of citrus like sunshine.
It wasn't all bad. Sometimes he liked it,
would pluck his eyebrows to reedy lines for
the Lemon Man, expression of surprise.

9

Morning after, I wake to find you gone.
In panic, I fail to hear the shower,

steam from the bath sewed with the fragrance
of exotic tinctures—apricot, star fruit.
Suddenly, it's too much. The familiar—
morning's pink hush, sparks of riffraff in light,
the sound of you one room over. Distinct
yet accessible. Joining you as you
lather the tableau of your chest, froth breathless at the tips of your hair, there is this
moment of nothing to say. I reach out,
dust the tip of a nipple. Sheepishly,
you grin. I've seen this a hundred times.
It decants my heart, like the first time, the last.

10

In the dresser mirror, flashing lights from
neon outside dress the room in pinks, blues.
Sable packs her things as queens turn their prize,
inflamed faces into view of the glass.
Michael rubs his hips like magic lamps.
Effects are startling, how so little can do
much. *Look at this*, he says. *Hourglass!*
He walks to me, waist rolling like a rough sea—
and it's as if he's real for the first time
under his skin. My chest half-lifes to dark
matter, the something that's always nothing—
love, loneliness, guilt. Sable turns to leave,
and I run to plead for that needle,
for spaces within me needing to be filled.

Dead Leg in Heaven
Stephanie N. Johnson

When you get to heaven
the leg waiting for you
will be walking proudly
in the limb community center.
It will be wearing
a badge with your name
printed on it,
but will be the wrong size,
perfect only for an ax
handle, if this is any consolation.
You'll embrace
the fragment of your flesh
both recalling a memory
you shared—the barn dog
who dragged home the severed
leg of a deer one cold winter.
You might even laugh
together like the first joke
between a father reunited with his son.
Of course, you'll want to avoid
rekindling that moment
of awkward separation.
He won't be wearing
the shredded strip of denim
he died in.
Instead, look for

clean white linen,
a wreath of clover blossoms
around the knee.
All this to conceal
the rapture—
those splintered fibers
like a crackling grass fire
that's already moved
into the trees.

❋
VANISHING SARAH
Maureen A. Sherbondy

BIT BY BIT Sarah vanished. It began slowly—a swatch of fingertip tugged off.

Everyone wanted something: her five children, her corporate husband, the in-laws, the neighbors, her two terriers, the PTA, her four younger sisters, the church parishioners. They were the takers, and she was the giver; this is the way it had always been. She barely noticed the initial throb of missing fingertip. The dull pain was interrupted by the disappearance of the small toe on her left foot, removed by her husband. Then, an ounce of flesh above her hip, which, really, she didn't mind, as there had been so much extra flesh since that fourth pregnancy. The removal of flesh was like being gnawed by a very large rat. Chomp chomp. First she swatted the hand of the taker, a PTA parent this time, then she accepted this loss and waved goodbye as the ounce of flesh floated out the open window.

Phones rang endlessly with additional requests: to bake two dozen cupcakes for the school bake sale, volunteer for the book fair, organize the church charity talent show. Then the takers became ruthless. They descended, a swarm of hands and teeth. A finger, wearing her wedding band, floated away from the four-bedroom brick house, and then a large toe left the suburban cul de sac. Her slightly bulbous nose sprayed with tiny freckles drifted into the sky, which made smelling the burning cupcakes difficult.

At night, achy, feeling scattered and lost, she closed her eyes (still intact, she had covered those with palms, no fingers) trying to find a dream where only givers lived. But, piece-by-piece even dreams parted.

When the children and husband and in-laws and PTA and church parishioners searched for Sarah, to ask *just one last little favor*, all that remained was a stain—a perfumed outline of who she had been.

❋
READING JAY'S MIND
Jeannette Brown

"WHAT DO YOU WANT?" Sylvia's breath carried the words into the stuffy hospital room, moving the air only slightly.

"Why do you have to know now? Today? There's plenty of time." Jay turned over so that his back was to his sister. End of conversation. His thin blue hospital gown gaped open at the back, but he ignored the chill.

"When do you think would be a good time to discuss this?" Sylvia shredded the tissue in her hands.

"When it's time. I'll let you know."

"Great. I'm sure you'll come out of denial just before you go incoherent. Perfect." She didn't mean to badger him but it would all be on her, and she wanted it to be right. She couldn't get it right without him. This banal hospital room with smiling, helpful attendants coming in and out was not conducive to a heart-to-heart. Or serious planning. Or funeral planning. Did he want a funeral? A memorial service? Actually, those are for the living, so perhaps he should not be consulted at all. But such things can be the epitome of the "loved one's" personality, the last mark they make on the world. His final statement about life should not come from her.

She hadn't seen him much in the past five years, since he had moved to California. Phone calls, an annual visit, but she knew there were things he didn't tell her, his big sister: loves gone bad, failed businesses. His apartments. He moved often and on some trips she never even saw where he was living. His blond hair was thinning, maybe because of the meds. He was terribly thin, which was to be expected. But his green eyes were still sparkly, and he still used his hands to reiterate what he was saying.

When he was little—say, nine—his favorite hymn was the one about

His eye on the sparrow. Was that the name? But that was twenty years ago. He must have a new favorite hymn. She had been through several herself.

"What's your favorite hymn these days?" she asked.

" 'Walkin' After Midnight,' the Patsy Cline version."

"Very funny. How do you feel about 'Amazing Grace' played on the bagpipes?"

His right hand dismissed the idea. "It's been done. Overdone."

"What about 'Will the Circle Be Unbroken?'"

A derisive snort. "Oh, fine. The adult version of 'Kumbaya.'"

"Remember when we used to stay with Gram in the summers and she'd take us to all those funerals? Some old pillar of the community would die, and we'd go to the First Baptist Church at two o'clock. The choir would be there and we'd sing all those great hymns." Sylvia remembered her childhood awe of grownups and their ways. "The women in black, long hot black dresses cooling off with those paper fans flapping the air in sync. We didn't think a thing about those fans being supplied by the funeral home." Sylvia looked to see if Jay was laughing. It was hard to tell by looking at his back. "Afterwards, we'd go to the cemetery for more prayers and hymns. Those were great funerals."

"Isn't it ironic that they went out of style before Gram died?" he asked. He was the irony expert. "She outlasted most of those old people. Only about four showed up for her. And it was in that so-called chapel in the funeral home, where they played that horrible taped music."

She wished he would turn around. She resisted the impulse to thump him somewhere vulnerable by focusing on the corner of the medicinal green room. "Gramps asked for her favorite songs," she explained, "but they weren't on the tapes so she got whatever they played." She smoothed a wrinkle out of her skirt. "But she got the last laugh. She wasn't even sick when she went to the funeral home and picked out that emerald green dress to be buried in."

"Poor Gramps." He rolled back a little, more toward her. "He helped everyone in town, especially the widows who couldn't get to the store for groceries. But when he finally went, there was that terrible blizzard. No one could get to that awful funeral home to watch us grieve." He was warming to this.

She kept it going. "Remember the four of us—you and me, Mom and Sam—cooped up in Gramps' house for days, trapped by the storm, eating cold cuts, sorting through all their stuff? It was barbaric."

"Speaking of, where are Mom and Sam?"

Sylvia took a deep breath. "They're home. They'll come out in a few... weeks." She couldn't tell him that their mother refused to believe Jay was dying and their stepfather refused to believe Jay was dying of AIDS. Maybe a funeral would convince them.

She got back to the subject. "What about your stuff? Who gets what?"

He flipped back toward the wall.

"Jay. You have to decide. I can't. Your friends will read something into everything I do and assume it's on your behalf, that that's the way you wanted. It's the last thing they'll remember about you. Do you still have that rug, the oriental? And the piano? Who do those go to? Have you written all of this down somewhere? You've had time to think about this. What did you decide?"

"Isn't this one step removed from grave robbing? My things are just things. Take them to Goodwill or a consignment shop."

"Cute, but not an option. You have some very special things—some because of their actual worth but mostly because they were yours. We could dump it all, but that would really ruin the market in say, silver. You wouldn't want that."

"Sylvia, when the time comes—and I'll let you know when that is— I'll make a list. Like when George and I split up. We made a list: 'you get the Victrola, I get the sewing machine, you get the Ford and the payments, I take the old Buick.' It'll work out. There's time."

But that's not true. The doctor had said two weeks to a month. Jay knew that. Did he believe the doctor? Maybe he felt that this was not the end, that there was more time or a new drug that would help. Or maybe he just did not give a damn who gets the armoire. And why should he, when he was facing this leap into the unknown?

After a tap on the door, a nurses' aide came in with a huge glass vase of calla lilies. Sylvia checked the card. *See you soon, somewhere. Love, Fredrick.*

The name sounded familiar but not recent. "Fredrick sends his best."

"That's not much," Jay laughed. "He lives from rehab to rehab. He'll probably die soon of id overexposure."

At least Fredrick was not in denial. Sylvia set the vase on the bureau with the other flowers from friends known and unknown to her. No pot plants, just a bank of cut flowers in all of nature's shapes and scents and colors.

"Jay, what's your favorite color? Not for any reason, just that it used to be green. Is it still?"

"No, after green, there was an orange period. Then red. Vibrant, regal, rich red the color of blood. Sarcomas. But now I'm into pastels. The rainbow is my favorite color."

"Are you being inexact on purpose?"

"Maybe."

"This is frustrating. I'm going downstairs for a cup of coffee. You nap. Maybe when I come back, you'll be in the mood to help with this."

"Fine." He always said "fine" like it wasn't.

Sylvia picked up her purse and walked toward Jay's bed. She touched him lightly at the base of the neck where he used to be ticklish.

She took the elevator to the basement. Even though the coffee shop was noisy, it was possible to hear people talking under their breaths about sickness and dying, with occasional general gossip interspersed to distract from the obvious. The doctors and nurses and orderlies sat apart from the patients and their visitors so as not to offend them when the staff discussed national football scores and personal golf scores.

Sylvia bought a cup of black coffee and backed through the door to the side yard where she could smoke. The medium-size cup would yield a two-cigarette coffee.

She felt guilty about smoking. It was offensive, even to her. It looked like a public death wish. Jay would love the irony—he, slowly dying of AIDS and she, probably dying even more slowly from cigarettes.

She had never considered designing her funeral or writing her will. Of course everything would go to Jay, except now there would be no Jay. It would be macabre to leave her things to Larry. Rooms full of reminders of her to the man who had moved on to a new love. Things had just accumulated, special only to her, and she remembered the story behind every purchase, every souvenir, every gift.

People planning suicide usually start giving things away. No one realizes what's going on 'til Joe blows his head off in his house, empty except for one chair.

If she got a disease, instead of death-by-car-wreck, maybe she'd have a little Open House near the end with special friends invited over to "take what you need and leave the rest." And for the funeral, she could buy a "pre-need" package, pick out the casket, designate a few hymns and a poem, and let the details sort themselves out.

Sylvia lit another cigarette. Comfort. Funny how the enemy often gives comfort.

Chocolate. Scotch. Sex. Lovers.

She ground the cigarette out under her shoe, plopped it into the coffee and threw it all in the trash bin. She hadn't noticed how good the fresh air smelled until she opened the door to go back into the hospital. As she passed by a table of people wearing scrubs, she heard an authoritative voice say, "...help the living to live and the dying to die. Or vice versa."

She took the stairs up three flights, pushed open the door to Jay's room, and said, "Jay.

Wake up."

"I'm not asleep."

"You were supposed to nap."

"No, that was your idea."

"Jay. Why don't you come to my house for Thanksgiving? You can teach me to make a turkey and all that stuff. We can shop for the pans and ingredients."

"That's two months away. I don't know what I'll be doing then. I may start a new business or fall in love."

"Okay, we'll set the table for three. Four. We'll invite Larry.

Jay sat up. "What's with you?"

"I don't know. I was trying to plan your funeral. And it wouldn't plan. So now I'm planning a party. A holiday. What do you say?"

"Fine. What's your favorite hymn?"

Eucharist

David E. Joyner

I am a fallen target,
Tattered, torn and tagged
Zipped into a bag
A metal wafer on my tongue
The taste of rusty blood

Boxed and gift-wrapped
Beneath a coverlet of Stars and Stripes
Folded into a triangle
Presented by white-gloved hands,

Then guns, a shammed salute
As if I'd not heard them, or
Known their dirty work

This is my body
   Broken for you
      Sold for a barrel of oil

SEATING ARRANGEMENT

Kory Wells

The homeless man
on a 6th Avenue bench
looks me up and down
and tells me I am
fine.

The man at home
in the leather La-Z-Boy
if he looks at all
tells me I am
not
what I used to be, a fact

hard as the bench,
but I am fine
with my forty-year-old seat
a bit overstuffed with life.

�֍ CHILDBIRTH

DeeDee Agee

IT WAS 1968, and I was twenty-one, pregnant, and on the brink of life. For the first time I could remember I felt like a whole person with a reason for being on earth.

I sewed two tent-like corduroy jumpers and wore them with the antique lace and embroidered blouses I'd been buying for years in second-hand stores. Having been made for the smaller women of a bygone time, they were too short-waisted. Intending to make them over someday, I'd never worn most of them, and now, amazingly, they were perfect under those jumpers. I loved the feel of luxury, the see-through veil of white cloth, the weight of intricate embroidery lying on the skin of my arms. I bought a pair of navy wool sailor's pants and changed the way I buttoned the front panel flap so as to accommodate my expanding middle. I'd never felt so at ease in my clothes, so at home in my body, myself. All my life I'd stood before my closet in the mornings finding nothing that seemed right, and now suddenly with just two jumpers I had a wardrobe I loved.

I liked the look of my skin when I was pregnant. It seemed to have a resiliency, an added depth and tone I'd never seen before. I found I walked in a new way, straighter and at the same time freer, less tight. Walking down the street, my arms swung loose from my shoulders. I found a grace I didn't know I possessed that even as I grew bigger seemed to blossom. Just sitting on the subway or on the couch at my mother's or at the formally-laid dining table at Bill's mother's, or in my literature seminar at Columbia—just sitting, I felt at ease with my body, with my physical presence in space. Like the feeling of relaxing in a sauna. I knew what I was doing. I was growing a baby inside of me, a new life. I liked myself. On the subway or walking down the street or at night at the bar in Max's Kansas

City drinking ginger ale, I felt that everyone knew what I was doing, what I was there for. No one ever asked me what I did anymore.

At night I lay in bed trying to feel the first stirrings of life inside me, to feel them from the inside. I would imagine the most delicate internal rumblings to be the baby moving. I lay with my hands on my belly, trying to feel life from the outside too. Later, my belly swollen out, I looked over my shoulder at my reflection in the mirror; there were two rounded places protruding, one on each side of me where my waist used to be. Someone said when you stick out more at the sides than in front you're going to have a boy.

I sat in the canvas butterfly chair in my white cotton nightgown like an egg in an eggcup. I pulled the cloth of the nightgown tight, and watched the lumps move across my belly making the skin bulge out in one continuous movement like a mole digging underground. I'd place my hands lightly over a moving lump and try to guess whether it was an elbow or a foot pushing outwards, to picture the whole tiny body turning inside. Like a blind person feeling a face. I remember the feeling of movement underneath the tight skin, the strangeness something pushing outwards from within me that was not me.

At night I filled the bathtub about one third of the way full, and as I lowered my body into the hot water, it rose to surround me on all sides. My rounded sides slid against the sloped sides of the bathtub. Eventually I couldn't get out without Bill's help. He'd grab me under the arms from behind and hoist me while I used my arms to brace myself on the rim of the tub. Then he dried my legs and feet since I couldn't reach them anymore. He treated me like a little girl; that was the only way he knew to be tender.

I loved to look at the baby clothes which lay in folded stacks, neatly lined up in a freshly painted closet with striped paper on the shelves. I'd unfold the tiny undershirts and hold them up to my belly trying to picture a baby that small inside me, trying to feel what it would be like to hold someone that small outside of me in my arms. I couldn't imagine a human being that small. I loved to fold and stack the clothes, to hold them to my face, to feel and smell the cool freshness of them, the newness. Through these clothes in their piles I imagined my day-to-day life, dressing, undressing, washing, drying, folding, stacking. I never told anyone I did this.

I went to the clinic at New York Hospital. I couldn't afford a private obstetrician, and they had natural childbirth classes and rooming-in so you could have the baby in the room with you, an innovation at the time. I imagined I'd have an easy time giving birth, being a big woman from east European peasant stock who pushed their babies out by the sides of fields and went right back to harvesting.

In the natural childbirth class a dozen pregnant women shyly watched a slide show of a birth. We lay on the floor and practiced the different types of breathing. The husbands were supposed to come to the next meeting, but Bill said he wouldn't come. He didn't want to see the baby being born. He didn't think the father had much to contribute to the raising of a child until it could talk. I figured he would change his mind after the baby was born and was a real person in his arms.

At the clinic, I saw a different doctor each time. I waited half the morning on a molded orange plastic chair with other rounded women like me. I remembered at twelve how I almost couldn't believe it when my breasts began to develop, convinced as I was that I was so alien, so not like other girls, that I would remain flat-chested forever. When my own tender, matching swellings began to blossom forth, I was ecstatic; I too was subject to the laws of nature, and was, like every woman, to be the owner of breasts.

The last couple of months I got the same Indian doctor a few times in a row. He was short and slight and seemed in awe of the hugeness of me. About a month before the baby was due the doctor said the head had descended into my pelvic basin, and that this meant the baby would most likely be born early, as much as three weeks early.

As it turned out, the baby was born exactly three weeks late.

Those last six weeks I did things to make the baby be born. I sat atop the rumbling vibrations of the engine back and forth on the Staten Island ferry, bounced all over the city in Bill's panel truck with no springs, spent two days on my hands and knees double-waxing the parquet floors in our seven room apartment on West Fifteenth Street. Our living room faced south overlooking a row of gardens which we shared with the buildings on either side. In the afternoons with the sun streaming in, I lay on the couch and stared out the window. It was very quiet. I'd dropped out of my classes at Columbia, except for a literature seminar with Carolyn Heilbrun, and finally I stopped going even to that. I always meant to go, but somehow when the time came I couldn't bring myself to move off the couch. I thought about names. Bill said Harley for a boy; I wanted Shane, Lily or Laura (my grandmother's name), for a girl. The last two weeks I lay on the couch most of the day absorbed completely, mind and body and soul, in our two bodies, the baby's and mine approaching together the moment of separation. I barely believed anymore that I was going to have a baby. Strangely, with each day I believed it a little less. Lying on that couch in the afternoon sun, I imagined myself, beached and in an advancing state of pregnancy through all eternity.

One night in bed there was some tightness across my belly and the small of my back. We timed the intervals between contractions; twenty minutes apart. We stayed up most of the night counting, but the contractions got weaker and farther apart and when it was light out I fell asleep for a couple of hours. The next night while I was cooking dinner they started up for real. Soon the lower part of my back felt tense to the point of being in spasm, as though there were wires attached to my muscles inside, all of them pulled taut to a central point. Soon it began in the front too, under my belly where I could no longer see, a pulling and tugging in great wrenching waves that made me double over. I lay on my side, my legs drawn up, my arms around myself, hugging. I realized it was the same position the baby was in. After five hours or so Bill took me to the hospital in the truck, but when the nurse examined me, she said I was only one centimeter dilated and told me to go home. "You have to get all the way to ten centimeters to get the baby out," she said. As though I didn't know that.

I waited around for awhile, hoping for a really bad contraction to convince them to admit me. I didn't want to have to ride all the way home again in the truck with no springs. But the contractions died down completely, and I could tell that the nurse thought I was a stupid, hysterical woman for coming to the hospital too soon, and I felt ashamed.

On the way home I tried to balance my weight on my arms over the bumps on the two stacked tires that had replaced the passenger seat, but I kept slipping into the center hole. Back home, curled into myself, I threw up in a plastic waste basket next to the bed. In my mind was a picture of a spear pressed to my belly pushing through my flesh, breaking the skin and touching the innermost center of my body with its sharp point. After it had touched my center, and I had breathed and withstood it, I would throw up again in the bucket until there was nothing left to come up and I was just heaving. The baby was very quiet. Not like at night when he would move a lot, and I would feel him pushing out the taut flesh of my belly here and there and the soft rumblings of his whole body shifting inside me, turning. I couldn't feel him now, only the sharpness of pain. I wondered what he was feeling, whether he was a boy, what he looked like, and who. When he was ten I would be thirty-two. Bill would be forty-one.

Bill kept falling asleep, and I told him to call my mother. She finally came and sat on a kitchen chair beside the bed, and suddenly I was crying very hard, like a kid, my nose running all over, and I said I didn't think I could stand it much longer. She sat stiff on her chair and said, "Well, Deedee, you just have to," and I thought how she must be thinking that I am disgusting with vomit and tears and a baby coming, nothing but a big dirty baby myself.

At eight in the morning, my mother and Bill took me back to the hospital in a cab. The nurse said I was only three centimeters dilated, not enough to be admitted. I started to cry, told them I hadn't slept in two days, and in the end, they said okay, but I should be prepared that the baby probably wouldn't be born for another day. I lay for a long time alone in a small cubicle with a green curtain pulled shut for a door, and then a very black-skinned lady in a green hospital gown came in with a basin and gently shaved me, just the two of us in the room, and she talked softly, and I didn't want her to go away.

They took me upstairs on a wheeling stretcher to the labor room. On my back the ceiling lights passed over me regularly like headlights of on-coming cars. The labor room was pale green and had elevator music piped in and a framed landscape on the wall like a motel room. I heard a nurse say they were so busy that day they didn't know where they were going to find beds. They took my clothes and shoes, everything but my wedding ring and glasses. There was a plastic bracelet on my wrist, but I couldn't remember when I had gotten it. They gave me a green gown like the one the woman who shaved me had worn and put me in a high bed with a railing like a crib. Another nurse came and stuck an IV in my arm; she hung the bottle on a metal rack attached to the bed. From somewhere a woman screamed in Spanish, and I promised myself I wouldn't scream, wouldn't give them the chance to look at me like a weak person. I breathed with the contractions then, forcing air into my lungs, counting time and letting out the air, my breath a weapon against the pain.

A nurse came in and said it was time for my enema. I told her I hadn't eaten or drunk anything in twelve hours and that I had been throwing up all night, but she didn't listen. She smiled through everything I said and never looked at me.

"Turn on your side, dearie." I had never had an enema. It felt like my bowels were being torn out. "Ring when you're through, and then hubby can come up," she said as she left. I tried to balance my egg-shaped body on the stainless steel bedpan, but I kept toppling part way off, and then I'd start to laugh, but it hurt too much and it turned to crying. It seemed like it took two hours for the hot liquid to leave my body, and the wrenching pain of each contraction made me sweat and shiver. After a while the nurse came back. She sprayed the room with air freshener, "For the doctor," she whispered, and winked. She took the bedpan and draped a crisp white towel over it, carried it away like a waitress. I felt acutely, overwhelmingly at their mercy; at the mercy of enemas, IVs, bedpans, and any other needless torture they cared to put me through. Like in nightmares when you scream and no sound comes out. I had no voice. They wouldn't listen to me. I was less than a child to them. My body no longer was mine; it had been taken over by the baby, by the hospital, by the pain. It went on and on, the wrenching of my guts, the shattering of my center inside. I felt I was in mortal combat with the baby.

Suddenly there was a change. The spear was gone, and now a large metal plate like the ones they use to cover holes in the street pressed down on my abdomen, squashing me down so that my insides felt flattened against my back. Then Bill was there and I held his hand and cried.

They gave me a shot of Demerol which made me sleepy and made it harder to think clearly and keep track of the breathing. A doctor I didn't know stood between my legs and broke my waters then, and a warm flood of liquid burst from me. I felt embarrassed for Bill. He'd never looked at me there between the legs. Then I realized that he was sitting by my head and couldn't see, and that I couldn't see either even though I seemed to be watching myself from above.

The contractions came closer and closer together so that it seemed like one long contraction with short periods of no contraction, and I saw behind my eyes an image of the baby's head, huge and leaden, pushing mercilessly against my bowels, squashing them, squeezing out the oxygen from all the tissues of my body, and again there were great wrenching piano wires pulling in all directions at my insides, and then all at once I felt like I had to shit a watermelon, and I knew this was the second stage of labor, and I rang for the doctor. He lifted the sheet, and I heard him say, "Whoops, the head is crowned," and there was a tinge of panic in his voice, and suddenly the air sucked out of the room and the nurses were rushing here and there, "born any minute now," I heard, and the pain overwhelmed me. I'd been prepared for hours more, and suddenly it was minutes. I forgot all about breathing, and with the next contraction, I felt like I was going to die, and I screamed out to do something, give me something, anything just make the pain stop please!, but they were wheeling me out of the room right in the bed, and I saw Bill getting smaller, left behind, and I wondered if I couldn't meet his eyes because I didn't have my glasses on or because they weren't there to be met, and they wheeled me fast down corridors of light and there were screams all around, and then I realized they were my own screams even though they sounded like they were some other woman's screams coming from some other woman's mouth, because somewhere it wasn't me this was happening to, except that I could feel all the pain as though it really was.

Just when I felt like the weight of a building was pressing on my belly and bowels, like the biggest press in the world was pinning me on the table, pushing me into the center of the earth, just then somebody said, "Lift," and gave me a little pat on the thigh to say I should lift my torso a few inches up onto some other table, and I just laughed at them—couldn't they see there was a building on top of me?—and they said, "Do you want to have the baby in the bed?" and I screamed, "Yes, yes, just make this stop, please." And then somehow—I really don't know where they got the strength—some of them lifted me up under the round light, and they took my two legs which were no longer attached to me and draped them over cold metal behind the knees, and tied them there with leather straps with buckles, and they belted my wrists to the sides of the table too, and then something came down to my face like a toilet plunger, and they fitted something heavy and cold over my nose and mouth, and I felt like there was no space inside of me for there to be air to keep me alive, and they said to just breath naturally. All of a sudden there was something new, and all I knew or could feel was that I wanted to, needed to *push* more than anything in the world, that if I pushed maybe the building would not press down on me so hard, maybe there would be space for air to come into my lungs, though there really was no choice one way or the other, and I pushed and they screamed, "Don't push, don't push, you'll tear yourself," but I didn't care what they said, if I did, didn't believe them or care anyway, couldn't have stopped if I did, and I pushed and pushed, hoped I would die, which would be fine if only the pain would please stop. I felt something, someone there between my legs then, heard the snip of scissors, the sound of cutting, but not the pain, and I felt the building move down a little, the press ease up, and I heard someone say, "the head."

Next thing I knew my eyes opened to that bright circle of light over me. The building was gone, my arms and hands were free, air filled my chest. Someone said *congratulations, a healthy boy, eight pounds, ten ounces.* I said, *Let me see him,* but he'd already been taken away to the nursery.

THE FUNNY
Richard Remine

BIRDS IN WINTER

Judy Loest

Hokusai's crane stares down
From my bedroom wall
Graceful on his icy bough
Like the doves outside in snow.

These January mornings are truth
Laid bare, a cold combustion
Of white winnowing earth
And air. Even the sparrows

Have fallen, tucked round
And still as stones
While the earth takes back
Its dead. A single crow

Skims the grizzled hair
Of kudzu along the river,
Vanishing in hoary smoke.
There is no hiding here

In this unforgiving season,
In the silent stare of sparrow
And dove unimpaired
By guilt or reason.

Nothing reminds the body
Of its simple needs or place
In the inscrutable hurl of time
Like the stillness of birds in winter.

On Ferry Road

Carole Borges

I keep remembering how mysterious
the world seemed, the day you taught me
seagulls always point into the wind.

It's too bad, Dad, that you never got to
see yourself laid out in that cold
New England funeral parlor.

Eyes closed, hands—.
the ones the Parkinson's made twitch
like two hexed divining rods searching for water—
white as wax they were, still as unlit candles.

I'll never forget that day on Ferry Road,
trying to give you a bath,
fumbling with the zipper on your pants.

As your knees buckled, your torso twisted.
Your hands flew to cover what they could not cover,
the boney buttock, the shriveled scrotum.

I thought—*I came from there!*
I came from there!

Then, the room became a wave
and you and I were riding fast.

Seeing Elizabeth Murray's Work at the Museum of Modern Art

Deborah Scaperoth

We return to Thebes no matter what.
And when you think you've found
the right road, your body
takes you back to the city gates.

In a plane over New York,
my grown daughter talks about choices
as I try not to notice our chewed nails,
wishing desperately she'll end up
with the right mate, the right life.

Silent but listening, I am distracted.
A woman's unringed hand across the aisle
holds a crochet magazine with pictures
of white filigreed patterns,
a pink thumb carefully manicured.

Elizabeth suddenly tells me
about a young friend with a deadly
lymphoma. Just diagnosed.
He's at home playing X-Box 360
as imploding cells fight it out.

She launches into new theories
of art in which painters replicate
the ways the brain sees life

focusing on one or two objects
in the foreground, the rest softly blurred.

Later at the museum, she observes
how Murray's paintings involve
all the clichés of sex.
I tell her they're about cancer.

WHAT WE WERE WEARING
L.A. Hoffer

AUNT VIRGINIA STAYED. I had a bad habit of telling lies, and that's what I was doing when her truck pulled up to our house on Folly Beach. I stood by the tide pools and told this red-haired boy that the real reason my father wasn't around was because he spent half of every year in California, swim-coaching Olympic hopefuls. It could've been true; the man Mother said had atrocious handwriting and liked to shrimp off piers had, in fact, been a swim coach. The red-haired boy was a tourist's kid, anyway; he'd be gone in a week. He just stared at our house: pre-Hurricane Hugo, peeling stilts, ripped mosquito netting around the back porch. When my mother appeared on our boardwalk and called for me to help Aunt Virginia unload her bags, the kid turned around and ran toward the ocean, yelling, "I swim better than you do!"

My mother had a bad eye from a botched nasal operation that would leak tears in the sunlight, so she wore sunglasses; her eyes were invisible. I wore a bikini and sand—sand in my hair, in the crooks of my elbows, stamped in waves on my belly. Mother frowned and said, "Help your aunt unload, why don't you? And don't tell her any little fibs." I didn't know Aunt Virginia. The day before she arrived in June 1980, all that my mother told us was, "She's been living in Germany, and now she's back, and she's my sister. Outside this house, you call her Virginia, you hear? Not aunt. Not that."

I walked barefoot on the gravel drive to Virginia's pick-up truck. She wore jeans and a man's V-neck undershirt. She wore six hoops in one ear and seven in the other; I counted them right away. I don't remember now which ear had more hoops. "Gail, right?" Spilling dirt, she dropped a spider plant on the driveway. Then she kicked a box toward me, full of

Roman candles, bottle rockets, and extra-long sparklers, all the labels in German. "You want these?"

"Don't tell Mom," I said. Virginia wiped her hair, and when she smiled, she bit her bottom lip as if she had to stop up a huge joy.

My older sister, Kieley, had to give her bedroom to Virginia and move into my room. I spent that entire summer in my bathing suit. By early August, it was typical for me to wake up to Kieley smacking me in the face with a pillow, saying, "There's sand in the sheets! Would you put on some clothes and get out of that stinking bikini?"

I pretended to still be asleep while she turned on the radio to a broadcast of the latest hurricane watch. A tropical storm was wheeling up the coast toward Charleston again, and the meteorologist said it might land on us this time at Folly Beach. "That's the third time this summer that dip's said that," Kieley said. She cut off the radio, sat down at the mirror and smeared on purple lipstick. She thought she was adult because she was sixteen, wore satin underwear, and showered three times a day.

Slammed drawers echoed in the hall; Mother was inspecting Aunt Virginia's dresser. She used to do that to Kieley and me too—rummaged through our stuff for *contraband*—and left whatever she found sitting neatly on top of our beds, so I'd stashed the fireworks in an old box marked "DOLLS" on top of my closet. But, when Mother searched through Aunt Virginia's things, it shut us up. I guess we'd never thought she would do that to another adult, especially her sister. When Mother came out of Aunt Virginia's room that morning, she hung one dark blue and one scarlet red bra on the doorknob. Her Roper Hospital nurse's uniform of thin, emerald-colored pants and smock was freshly ironed and pierced with a nametag—*Joyce Singer*—her maiden name. She pointed at the bras. "Virginia goes out at night. Did you know that?" she said. "I'm just sure she's doing gross things. Wait and see what turns up."

When I shrugged and ducked in the bathroom, Mother knocked on the door, called, "Gail, Mrs. Kroener stopped me in the street yesterday. Did you tell her that Virginia's in the Witness Protection Program?"

I spit toothpaste in the sink. Mrs. Kroener was our neighbor. That's it, I thought, Mrs. Kroener could eat a jellyfish before I walked her dog again. "No," I said, waiting for Mother to try and open the door.

"She says you did. One more lie and you're through swimming for the summer. I'll cut up all your bathing suits and throw them in the garbage disposal."

Virginia sat on a lawn chair on the beach just behind the tide pools, wearing a black one-piece and a scarf tied over her short, black hair. She'd been with us almost two months, but I still didn't know her. She never asked us, like Mother, to be quiet or quit tracking sand in the house. And though she'd brought that pick-up truck full of new stuff, she stuck it all, except for her clothes, in a locked shed under the house. She wouldn't let us see any of it.

I sat down and buried my feet in the sand. Wind beat the ocean high as a chain-link fence. I said, "How come you never swim?" and she said, "I can't."

"I learned to swim when I was two. I don't know anyone who can't swim."

"It happens," she said. She wore cats-eye plastic sunglasses and a smile.

"Then why do you have on a bathing suit?"

"It's just more comfortable this way."

"We're going to have a hurricane. It was on the radio. We had two hurricanes last year," I lied. And, though I was talking to her, it was mostly an excuse to look at her. She was 26, 14 years younger than Mother, and never wore the same clothes together twice. While Mother was at work, she dressed us up. I was eleven years old; her clothes swallowed me. That summer, we wore A-line skirts and platform sandals, red China berry beads and black jelly bracelets, pink halter tops and ripped jean shorts, floppy berets, leg warmers and black spandex, white fishnet stockings, white lipstick, white eyeshadow, tear-drop clip-on earrings, faux pearl bracelets, lace gloves. Once, she cursed at my mother in German, and her lips wore the sharp words like a pair of Lee Press-On Nails.

I fiddled with the sand and worked around to telling Virginia, "Mom's going through your stuff. I just saw her."

"I know."

"You don't care?"

"It's her house. Besides, I left most of my stuff in Germany."

"I wouldn't leave my stuff behind anywhere," I said.

"You might. You never know. Who needs all that furniture? Tables? A bed?"

I didn't say anything. I stared at the ocean and imagined that—an entire bed dressed with quilts and pillows, sitting on a curb beside the trash cans.

"I did bring these," she said. She pulled her jeans off the beach towel and shook two stones out of the pocket. They were gray and quartz, but with specks of pink, shiny as nail polish. "That's what the beach is made of in Germany, stones and buried sand." I thought she was lying, but I didn't say so. She said, "You can keep those. I have more." The tide rose and dyed the sand ash-black. Virginia jumped up when the water swirled over her toes, said, "I'm just going to move my chair back a little ways."

While Aunt Virginia napped on the beach, I swam and waded out to the old Morris Island lighthouse. It was still only 1980, but already, the ocean was swallowing the lighthouse. The water surrounding its base climbed during high tide that afternoon, and waves had already swept away half of the lighthouse's wooden door. Once, Kieley and I swam to the lighthouse—a year or two before Virginia came—and hoisted each other up onto the lowest remaining step. Trapped water sloshed around our legs, and the stairwell smelled of mold and dead crabs. Barnacles scratched our feet. Because it was my idea, Kieley said, "If we fall through, I'm going to kill you."

Lighting equipment gone; only a clean spot remained on the floor where the beacon once stood, and the panes of glass surrounding the chamber were cracked or missing. The brown stone balcony extended far out over the water and was full of gulls' nests. Kieley leaned on the railing, but I wouldn't because I thought it would fall off. I hugged the walls of the lighthouse chamber. We watched phantom shrimp boats way out in the ocean, but they didn't move an inch. Kieley said, "The water looks short, doesn't it? Like you could row across it in no time." I had nodded even though she wasn't looking at me, and some gulls landed on the railing. It shook. Kieley didn't move. She said, "I think I see England."

I didn't go into the lighthouse that day with Virginia. I don't know what day it was, but I know it was August, some time after Folly Beach began to empty of tourists, some time before I started middle school, and I swam around the lighthouse in the shallow water and wondered whether Aunt Virginia would ever come out there. I floated on my back with a face full of sky until the waves shored me.

Folly Beach did not wear seashells, it wore jellyfish. Aunt Virginia said the storms brought them, but they were always there, dozens of bodies sunk like dimples into the smooth, wet sand near the water. More jellyfish floated in the first few waves. Even the dead ones could sting, but I liked to step on them while Kieley sunbathed and yelled at me to quit making a mess. I used her high heels to make holes in the jellyfish and lied to her: "I got stung by one last week, and it didn't hurt at all!" But, I was scared of them and anything else I might step on and hated the way I couldn't see through the ocean water. I wore old sneakers when I swam.

When I woke up the next day, Mother and Aunt Virginia were talking in the kitchen at the other end of the hall—I heard Mother say, "You just don't leave a husband like that." Virginia's voice, much softer, said, "Shh, shh, shh, you just don't know where we lived." I couldn't hear anything else. I didn't know why Mother cared, because she'd told us a hundred times that she *politely asked* our father to leave a few days before I was born, *because he didn't look happy enough*. Kieley only had one memory of our father—a cleaved-off picture of him holding a crab by the claw. She remembered his thick hand, the shirt he wore, but not his face.

I fell back asleep. When I woke up again, Mother was at work.

We took a portable radio out to the beach to listen for weather updates. The announcer said Tropical Storm Gabriella was gaining speed as it hurtled toward the Florida coast. By afternoon, the radio coughed warnings every half hour, and Kieley stopped dumping lemon juice on her hair when the sun disappeared. She was stretched out on this Citadel Academy blanket some cadet from downtown had given her, trying to tan, but mostly just freckling. She wore a bikini top with shorts because she had birthmarks on her thighs she didn't want anyone to see. Kieley stood up and shook her blanket out, yelled, "Every time I come out here, the weather goes to shit!" I told her *she* was the ugly one who scared off the sun, then Aunt Virginia folded her beach chair and told Kieley and I to put our stuff in the house. She said, "Your mom won't be home for hours. I'll take you for a drive." We hurried; Kieley and I almost never got to leave the beach when school let out for summer. I actually changed into pants and a t-shirt before we left the house. My bikini was fading from sun-bleach. Virginia drove us up Folly Road in her pick-up, all of us squeezed into the front. We saw boards go up over house and shop windows around Charleston. We drove to South Windemere and the Ashley River, past marsh and pluff mud. Men chopped down oak limbs so they wouldn't fall and crash through roofs. Spanish moss and leaves and branches choked the roads. The sky swelled opal-gray, but it didn't rain. The heat sealed us to the truck's vinyl bench.

"I'll drive," Kieley said. Virginia held the wheel with one hand: "Not a chance."

On our way back, we stopped at an Eckerd's, because Kieley swore she needed new eyeshadow. Aunt Virginia and I waited in the truck. "Did you have hurricanes in Germany?" I said. Aunt Virginia laughed. "No, there's only a sea there, not an ocean, and it's too cold. Plus, I didn't live on the water."

"Where'd you live?" I was still so young then, and we'd lived on Folly forever. I thought everyone lived near water.

"Berlin. West Berlin."

I did know about that, I knew about the Wall from a filmstrip at school with nothing but black images—guards, guns, barbed wire, hungry-looking dogs. I couldn't imagine Virginia living in those pictures. "Why?" I said.

"Why what?"

"Why did you live there?"

Aunt Virginia put her hands on the steering wheel, though the car was off. "I went there to look for your father, in the beginning. I didn't find him." I didn't even think before I lied, "My father is dead." I would have said more, made the lie bigger, say he was waterskiing and cut in half by a boat, but she cranked the car. On the way home, we hit a Siamese cat. I looked in the rearview mirror and watched its legs bicycle the air. Aunt Virginia said, "*Gesundheit.*"

My father stopped swimming when he left my mother; he sold his car, his boat, began to travel. Virginia had chased my father to Germany when she was eighteen years old, and after he disappeared behind the Wall into the East, she decided to wait. After Virginia died, I broke the lock on the shed under the house and opened all the taped boxes of her things, and I found the letters addressed to Mrs. Virginia Schreiber instead of Miss Virginia Singer and posted just a month before she moved in with us at Folly Beach. When I finally wrote to Otto Schreiber years later, he sent me old photos of Virginia and himself standing in front of a train in West Berlin, holding their two year old son, Lukas, two weeks before he drowned in Lake Lietzensee, not far from the Wall or the Brandenburg Gate. When she had met and married Otto, she thought she'd live in Germany forever, but when her son drowned, she rode with his body in the *Ambulanzwagen*, left him on the coroner's table, took a train to her apartment, picked up her passport, and boarded a plane for the States before Otto even got home from work. Years later, when I flew to Germany and met Otto Schreiber, I said Virginia died in a boating accident. I have not stopped lying since; each lie hangs on me like a necklace.

Rain split the sky and began falling hard as emeralds by four o'clock. When Mother came home—early—Kieley had a ton of new makeup on her face. She held Kieley's chin and pointed it at Virginia, said, "Why does my daughter look like a little tart?"

"Mom—" Kieley said, but Mother hushed her. I'd been playing in the tide pools in the rain before she got home. I wore my bikini again, a towel wrapped around me like a strapless dress, and Aunt Virginia held me in front of her, stroking my hair. "Kieley's just playing dress-up, Joyce," she said. "She didn't leave the house like that."

"I came home to tape windows against who-knows-what storm, and look what I find. Go wash," she said and pushed Kieley toward the hall. Mother sat down, sighed, shook her head. "I don't enjoy this. She's got enough boyfriends without your help."

"Why don't you go to your room, Gail?" Virginia put a hand on my shoulder.

Mother said, "I can send my own children out of the room."

Virginia held up her hands, laughed. "Sorry. She didn't do anything wrong."

"Really? All she wants to do lately is everything you do." Mother turned to me. "Isn't that right, Gail?"

My wet hair dripped on the rug. "No, ma'am. Virginia just sits on a beach chair all day and won't even swim."

Mother sniffed like she smelled something bad. "Gail has a little problem with the truth," she said. Mother called everything *little*, as if living beside the ocean diminished the true size of things.

Later that night after all the windows were taped, all the rugs covered in plastic, I watched Kieley get ready to sneak out of the house. She put on a blue skirt and sat on the windowsill, holding high-heeled sandals, reeking of Virginia's White Shoulders perfume. "George," she said, "is having a hurricane barbecue. Tell Mom I went on a walk to the pier, if she asks." Then she crawled out to the porch and was gone.

By the time Mother let me back in the den to watch television, Aunt Virginia's truck was missing from the driveway. I flipped between *Gilligan's Island* and the Weather Channel, sitting on the couch with my nightgown pulled over my knees. When Mother patrolled the hall on her nightly check and realized Kieley and Virginia had left, she stormed in the kitchen and started making okra soup. Steam got in Mother's bad eye, and it began to leak. Around eleven, I asked if she was going to go to bed, but she said, "I'm waiting up. Someone's got to. But, I want you to go to bed, right now."

I made myself stay awake, wanted to hear what would happen. I listened to the wind suck at the windows until they squealed. The walls creaked so bad I didn't know Kieley had come in until she turned on the light. Her lipstick was all gone. She crossed her legs and kicked off her sandals. "I saw Virginia parked on Harborview Road." Then she just sat and smiled for a minute.

"Who cares?" I said.

"They care because she was in the passenger's seat, genius. I saw they were parked right under the streetlight, and so I had George pass back by, and I saw the driver's door open, and some guy threw a liquor bottle up and broke the streetlight bulb out with it. Mom's right; Virginia doesn't care who sees her doing what."

"How'd you know it was a liquor bottle?"

"I knew. George said so, too." She put on her nightgown.

Later, I said, "It could have just been a Coke bottle. You don't know."

"Shut up, I know what I saw. It was too big for a Coke bottle, anyway."

I got up and closed the bedroom door. "She was with a man?"

"Yep," Kieley said, and I blurted, "Don't tell Mom."

"I won't have to tell," she said. "She'll find out. Virginia's not hiding it." Kieley grinned like she'd just bitten someone. "And soon, I hope. I want my bedroom back."

Of course, Gabriella dissipated and dissolved into the Atlantic hundreds of miles from Folly Beach. Before the water calmed, the ocean seesawed in the wake of the storm while the last of the tourists renting homes nearby piled onto the beach to watch the surfers catch the best waves. The water turned white and waves swelled; the ocean was a poltergeist. I found a hundred jellyfish embedded in the sand before I stopped counting.

Aunt Virginia wouldn't let us swim, but we walked up the beach. She had dressed up that morning as soon as my Mother left the house, and she wore a flesh-colored, see-through shirt, fine as fishnet, over her white bathing suit and a long white skirt. Behind her, I watched her skirt eddy and churn in the wind. The last of the rain blew sideways and fisted Virginia's bare neck, but she just stood watching a surfer, her hands holding her scarf where it was tied under her chin. Now, when I think of it, I want to know if anyone saw Aunt Virginia with us that day, if anyone ever saw her at all.

Mother called at six that night to say there had been a boating accident in the harbor downtown, and she didn't know when she would be home. Aunt Virginia came into our bedroom to talk to us for a while. She was still wearing the fleshy, see-through shirt, and we could see the outline of her nipples clear as mosquito bites. Kieley stared at her and said, "That shirt makes you look naked; it's the same color as your skin."

"You want to borrow it?" Virginia said.

Kieley shrugged and began to brush her hair. "Just stating a fact."

"How do you say, 'You are a stupid ninny,' in German?" I said, and Virginia responded, all the words meaningless and whispery as the swish of scissors. Then she said, "Where are those sparklers I gave you, anyway?" in English.

We wore no shoes. It was after eight o'clock, after low tide carried the water back to the ocean. We walked in the wet sand to the Morris Island lighthouse, Kieley and I in nightgowns, Virginia still in her clothes. It was almost dark, and the garnet sky had no flaws. Virginia tied her skirt up in a knot just above the knee, and when her legs hit the water, she linked her arm in mine. The inside of the lighthouse was dark as a squid's eye. I felt seaweed wrap around my leg and jumped. Virginia lifted us onto the lowest remaining step, and we felt our way to the top while watching our hands and feet to avoid the barnacles growing on the rotted wood. Behind me, Virginia said, "If you tell your Mother about this, she'll ship me straight back to Europe."

Kieley said, "So what else is new?" and scooted through the hatch at the top. The air was colder on the balcony, and through the haze, we could hardly see the water below. My eyes adjusted to the last spark of daylight, and I could see Aunt Virginia smiling.

Kieley opened the plastic bag and took out the boxes of sparklers, said, "Christ, did you know there's a gross here?" and Virginia handed her a Bic lighter and said, "We're not lighting 144 sparklers. Not tonight. Your mom would love it if I brought you home with half a leg." Virginia dealt out a sparkler to each of us. We were quiet and just watched the first batch spangle and burn slowly. Kieley dropped hers off the balcony to fizz in the ocean.

"Don't do that, sweetie," Virginia said. "It'll hurt the fish."

We lit a second round, and I leaned over the balcony railing. The sparklers shone red, blue, and green, and smelled like peroxide and bug spray as they burned. I walked around the circle and viewed all of the wash-out, our end of Folly Beach, peered at the lights shining from hotel rooms at the Holiday Inn half a mile away. I didn't know what time it was. The haze made my sparklers smoke, and I went back to Virginia. She kept lighting more and handing them to us in bouquets until I couldn't see anything beyond the balcony and ourselves. Virginia held her sparklers two feet in front of her body, face and shoulders lit behind them, hair-kerchief skipping in the wind. Her lips glowed pale as oyster shells. She bit her smile. "Isn't this the best, Gail?"

Kieley had something like nine sparklers going at once on the other side of the tower, shaking them away from her to watch the embers flip off the balcony, giggling.

"Here, take some more," Virginia said. I held them up against hers while we stared into the green and blue light. The sparklers bit the dark, and then I leaned out too far on the balcony, and the iron post bent in its socket, but I didn't scream. Some of the sparklers dropped out of my hand and fell into the ocean, and the rest I gripped tighter, elbows cocked back, ready to fall backwards. When I thought I'd hit the concrete floor, I hit Virginia's arm. A blue line rushed up the sleeve of her hair-thin shirt—there must have been some chemical in the fabric—and then it stopped for a second, like it had just been static electricity, but her chest began to stir with fire. She spread her arms, and I ducked because she still had sparklers in her own hands. Flame whipped down her other sleeve. Kieley, standing on the other side of the lighthouse chamber, did not see this, and I heard her still giggling to herself as the flame changed directions on Virginia's body, pooled at her neck, and caught the tail end of the scarf she wore over her hair.

WHEN WE BECOME LIGHT...
Laura Still

the glory of the sun will no longer blind
though its power shall increase

so we will increase, our strength amplify,
our vision magnify till things now invisible
become clear

spinning orbits of Jupiter's moons,
Saturn's rings, the busy interior whirl
of our own atoms shimmer
in our new eyesight

as energy, palpable as skin, expands like heat.
Not dispersed, but transformed we rise...

Siya hamb' eku khanyeni kwenkos,
Siya hamb' eku khanyeni kwenkos.

Skin Speaks

Sheryl Hill Sallie

My skin speaks ancient times
Appears in hieroglyphic images
My skin breathed and the world began
Was intact before time could be captured
into minutes&hours&seconds
My skin covered pharaohs&queens
Covered the hands of the pyramid constructors
It speaks intelligence
Was considered richly beautiful by all who would see it
It grew golden in the Egyptian sun
Listen to the sight of my skin

My skin speaks a vast continent
Stretched&gave birth to humanity
Ran free&happy with lions&giraffes
As drums pulsated between rain forests
My skin is Yoruba,Zulu,Tutsi,Ashanti,Bantu
Was powerfully rippling covering warriors
And bronzed men and regal women
It glistened beneath the orange sun
My skin raped and torn apart
Only to be put back together in foreign lands
Listen to the anguish of my skin

My skin speaks triumph in shackles
In the mouths of Middle Passage sharks

SKIN SPEAKS

In the ruins&ashes of bombs
At the ends of nooses of the hanging trees
At the tips of whips&firemen's hoses
My skin crowned King and then Xed out by secret men
My skin is a vessel of pain
My skin hated by some,feared by others,
and intimated by most
Listen to the strength of my skin

My skin speaks music
Soul-wrenching gospels holding secrets from masters
Jazz as varied as my skins
Blues the originator of all music that is
It speaks Mahalia Jackson/Marian Anderson/Billie Holiday/B.B. King/
Snoop Dogg
My skin stolen to cover blue suede shoes
My skin can wail,scat,moan,rap; create melodious melodies
My skin is an instrument

SHHH, listen, can you hear my skin??
Denied its true greatness buried between the
pages of history
Listen SHHH can you ; can you
Hear my skin???

1986 Tattoo Guy
Richard Remine

SWALLOWS

Beth Long

i.
she sucks her thumb
and seals within her mouth
all that she cannot swallow.

ii.
this was a torture she read about:
they force water down the throat
more and faster
til you pass out.
when you wake
they do it again.

iii.
swallow faster harder
the swirls of red swallow
as they swirl red down the bathtub
drain I am a mouth that empties a mouth
that bleeds red blood bleeding red
into me.

iv.
i wont eat.

v.
died dead I will get a knife and cut it out.
this afternoon. now. I bury deep
when she eats outside
my door you open
to make me watch swallow
is a bird that will never come again.

Sonnet to My Self

Kay Newton

Well, old gal, old bag of flesh and bones,
we're stumbling some now that we've come this far
together, and as old Bob Dylan sang once,
it isn't dark yet, but it's getting there.
The dusk at the end of the tunnel is in sight
and lately we've begun to understand
why Mother, when confronted with a flight
of stairs, would roll her eyes and bitterly complain.
Our own knees have started getting creaky,
our cold, bare, ruined other sections, too:
our skin's too dry, our nether parts too leaky;
we qualify "at risk" for shots for flu.
Still, what a privilege we count it to endure
our problems—they won't last long, that's for sure.

Mapmaker

Terri Beth Miller

I will be a cartographer of your face.
With my eyes, my lips, my hands
I will map the vivacious geography
That is world, is life, is prayer
To me.

I will begin at the Bavarian Black Forest,
The raven hair of your head,
Resplendent now that it is not sacrificed in devotion,
For even a god would be jealous
Of such lustrous prodigality.

My fingers pierce the profligate ebony
Like moonlit silver birch far from the city.

Next I raft the dark jetty of your brow,
The Great Barrier Reef that girds the treasures of your intel-
lect,
The storehouse of that keen and captivating intelligence
That first won me.

I set my seal upon this mesmerizing vault of personality:
Two kisses and I must go, for your eyes await.

They are dangerous and delicious.
Chocolate delights. Muddy La Brea tar pits.
I risk being forever consumed,

swallowed in the murky depths
Of your unfathomable stare.

But such sweets are irresistible,
And like a glutton I return ceaselessly
To the savor of your gaze.

I slalom the Mount Blanc of your patrician nose.
It is here that your profile wins honor,
In the reverential curve of that proud, high Alpine ridge.

I zealously memorize the degree of the angle,
Emblazoning the shape of that obliqueness on the atlas of
my heart.
Then I reach at last, like all steadfast explorers,
That which is Zion, is Atlantis, is Elysium to me,
The dream city of your honeyed mouth,
Offering relief and release
To a weary and heartsick traveler.

Here I linger,
At the oasis of your lips,
Where Eden is not fallen,
And salvation may be had for a taste.

My Father Eating Anger

Candance W. Reaves

My father's body
lies like a baby bird
on the gurney in the ER,
mouth agape,
waiting to be fed,
his hair a tuft of fluffy gray,
skin blue white and wrinkled.

He had his predigested goo today,
but no diligent mother fed him.
It was delivered by tube
directly
to his small intestine,
his last meal.

When his body could no longer
stomach his life of liquor and dissipation,
he began to feed on his anger,
spewing vitriol and bile
at those who came close.

Now he lies so still,
still
hungry,
mouth

open
wanting
what we could never give.

Failure To Communicate
Christina Schneider

I feel a strange need to be comforted.
I want to rewind
like on the Discovery Channel,
those flowers that they play backwards
blossoming inwards.
Folding into the bright warmth of the womb.
Which I can't really remember:
women who haven't carried a child
know nothing of their wombs except
the ache of the sea reminder,
so she's only a traitor to me,
an assassin poisoning my blood with wild thoughts
and drowning me in pain monthly.

I try to verbalize the thing about the flower,
but feelings like that can't live outside your head,
outside of your veins.
I could have simplified it and said something like,
"Break me,"
or "Hold me,"
but instead I tried to make you feel me,
which is always stupid and dangerous
and I don't know what I was thinking.
Or rather, I do.
But you didn't.
And I was too blinded by bloombright
to realize that you couldn't.

A TOUR THROUGH HELL

Don Williams

SLENDER AND ATHLETIC, platinum hair brushed back from tanned skin inset with eyes of bluish-white searing all they lit upon, Rev. Hamby leapt to the stage and paced across it. Then he turned—too much energy to contain—pivoted a step away from the lectern, placed ample fists on slender hips and looked into faces peering back in hungry trepidation— more than one hundred-fifty filling the hushed auditorium of Love Baptist Church.

"Tonight I'm giving you a tour through hell," he said with a smile, but we already knew that. It was on all the fliers—loud black letters on crimson stock stapled to telephone poles or glaring from storefront windows.

Now remember, children, this was a time when most of us hereabouts believed in hell as an actual lake of fire, a place as real as the palms of your hands, fried chicken on Sunday and Ed Sullivan's "really big shoooo." I'm talking 1967 in East Tennessee, when Kelly Sue, my next-door girlfriend was thirteen and I was twelve and hell was no metaphor. It didn't mean "separation from God" nor "loss of grace" nor "dying in the agony of guilt" nor anything of the sort, as the visiting evangelist assured us. Not that he had to. A kid with a good imagination could scare himself to death conjuring sensations of hell real enough to make a stoic squirm. On many a sleepless night I felt those fires burning, all through my body.

The conundrum was this: As fundamentalists, Kelly Sue and I were either hell-bound or heaven-bound. There was no third way, and even though we'd both had that washed-in-the-blood experience there was room for doubt as to whether it had taken hold, whether we'd gone all the way in surrendering our hearts and souls, pride and arrogance, secret shames and hidden desires. And if we hadn't surrendered those to Jesus, why child, then we were bound for hell.

All of which raised questions. How could you know for sure? How were you supposed to feel after having your sins washed away? I imagined a state of perfect peace, of blessed assurance, but such feelings of purity and exultation never came, not the evening I confessed my sinful state before the whole congregation, not the sunny day Pastor Clyde Carpenter baptized me in the Pigeon River, not that night as I tossed on my bed trying to get to sleep.

So maybe God wasn't listening. What if I spent the rest of my days going to church and putting on a "really big shooo"—performing good works and all the rest—only to come down to the end sin-scarred and hell bound?

Fears and delusions flooded my mind, mingling with ceaseless delirium of carnal thoughts, for oh how I lusted after Kelly Sue—her fair, lithe body with burgeoning breasts so sweet. And oh how desire, such desire, damned my immortal soul.

On the other hand, Baptists held an ace in the hole—a peculiarity of dogma that declared man was not saved by works but rather through grace. The doctrine held inherent beauty. No matter what sins I might commit in a lifetime, the possibility of being saved by the grace of God always remained. I'm talking about the deathbed confession, child. Just before my last gasp, even as hell's gates began to open, I might have one last opportunity to repent.

God would give me a new body then, imperishable, beyond carnal desire, in which to walk streets of gold. I would be perfect—like Adam in the first dawn of creation, like Jesus, like Hercules or Superman.

Of course, by age twelve, everyone raised in Love Baptist had heard the drawbacks to the deathbed strategy. I can yet name three without breaking a sweat.

First, it was possible God would harden your heart. That is, preachers let us know that it was possible to live so long and so mean outside God's grace that your heart would shrivel to the toughness of an acorn and your own pride might prevent your ever opening it to Jesus.

Second, you might never get that deathbed opportunity. You could be decapitated in a car wreck like that sexy movie star, Jayne Mansfield.

Or you could die in a nuclear attack—the Cuban missile crisis was still a recent memory—or be shot dead or lie in a coma, unable to confess. Such things happened every other day.

Third, it was possible to commit the Unpardonable Sin without even knowing it, and that's what worried us most. Kelly was always asking me what *that* sin could be, after Rev. Carpenter brought it up one Sunday. Daddy said it meant there was just one sin God could never forgive. He thought it was atheism. Obviously God couldn't forgive one who denied His existence—where was the willing heart?

Uncle Dewey, the choir director who'd lost the middle finger of his right hand in World War One—so that its nub tickled my palm each time we shook—disagreed. He allowed how lots of people questioned God, even wrestled Him. He said that before he went to war he got drunk once and called himself an atheist, hard as that was to believe. No, Uncle Dewey thought the Unpardonable Sin was blaspheming against the Holy Spirit. He'd heard a drunk do that one time as he staggered down the street. I tried not to speculate about the drunk's actual words from fear that I might slip up and blaspheme too.

One Sunday Rev. Carpenter sat in on our Sunday school class and we asked him about it. He said the Unpardonable Sin just might be suicide. How could you be pardoned for suicide? There was no time, say, between pulling the trigger and your soul shooting down to hell. He reasoned that if you died without time to ask forgiveness, why then there could be no redemption.

Nobody could name the Unpardonable Sin for solid certain and the problem was, a kid like Kelly could figure out all kinds of ways she might've committed it without even knowing it.

"How do you keep from blaspheming against the Holy Spirit?" she asked one day as we sat facing each other in our hideout in The Gullies. That's what we called the red clay hillside her daddy had clear-cut several years back. Only now was it filling with a forest of little scrub cedars.

We'd meet each Saturday at noon inside our own favorite cedar-scented gully covered by an old tree twisted and bent so low that it had survived the clear-cutting—and with our ankles interlocked, she'd offer her slender lips and neck for kissing and intertwine her nearly translucent fingers with my swarthy ones. She didn't do it often because such pleasures fed our mutual guilt, and we feared God would cleave us apart for all time if we went too far.

Still, I imagined my fingers unbuttoning her blouse and sometimes she'd let me go so far as to rest a hand on her knee. Occasionally we'd kiss and hug and caress until we could scarcely breathe.

At night I trembled in fear of such desire, but how I hallowed the memory of our first kiss, when she'd taken hold of both my hands, looked me in the eyes, swallowed hard and offered in a trembling murmur, "Lonnie, you can't do that, I'm a Christian," just before closing her eyes and parting her lips. I'd seen her open them just that way when taking communion, and it was in keeping with such a transforming miracle that she parted them now for me.

Later, she mostly just slapped at me playfully before letting me kiss her, and in the past few weeks there were times she'd just yawn and stretch in an exaggerated way before murmuring, "I'm tired, I'm going to sleep now," and lying back on a soft brown bed of needles, she'd close her eyes.

The first time she did that, I sat looking, uncertain what to do, but when she groped for my hand and pulled me to her side, I lay down and spooned her willowy body in mine. We were exactly the same height, and with my arms around her I felt every part of her against me and was moved in mysterious ways. Thus I had inklings of the fickle demons possessing her. Even before I knew what unlawful carnal knowledge was I'd daydreamed of Kelly tying me to a tree deep in the woods with the help of her big sister, Gail, and taking off my clothes against my will, as if that would absolve me of any guilt for what might follow, just as Kelly's pretend naps absolved her.

On this Saturday, though, she showed no signs of stretching and curling into my spooning embrace. Rather we sat on opposite cedar-scented banks with heads low.

"I'm serious, Lonnie," she said, pushing my hands away, "I've been thinking about it all week. How do you know if you've..."

"What?"

She said it through pearly clenched teeth. *"Blasphemed the Holy Ghost?"*

"I reckon you'd know it if you done it," I answered.

"Have you ever?"

"No, don't guess I have, why do you ask stuff like that?"

"Because *I might've*," she said and tears sprang to those large, periwinkle eyes. "Last night while I was trying to sleep *my mind* thought what it might mean to curse the Holy Ghost and these words came to me three times in a row. I couldn't stop them."

"What words?"

Her lips trembled as she caught her breath.

"I'll tell you, but it don't mean I'm really s-sayin' them."

"Well what were they?"

"You have to promise."

"What?"

"That when I tell you them you understand I'm not *sayin'* the words to mean them, I'm just telling you what I already said."

"Okay."

Fiercely she whispered, as if to wait another second would prevent the telling, "Damn you, Holy Ghost." She looked away, then back at me for a judgment, but I was speechless. "That's what I said, three times, even though I tried to block it out." In the face of my astonishment, she turned white and covered her eyes.

It would be years later, as medics pulled me from my first car wreck one ice-glazed night that I'd discover there's nothing more terrible than seeing pure horror cross the face of somebody taking a look at you. Yet even then I had an inkling of the terror I'd made Kelly feel, as her fingers clenched mine.

"Oh, Lonnie, I've blasphemed." And then she whispered the question that likely has come to the mind of most every Baptist at least once. "Am I going to hell?"

I hugged her then, held her perishable body tightly to mine, so that it seemed we were one fragile creature with two heads, two hearts beating together, and I knew I'd never want no other kind of body or mind, not that day, not next Sunday, not ever again no matter what I might say.

"No," I whispered fervently, "No you're not, no you're not, no you're not, no you're not, you can't help what you think," but she was crying and

I was blinking back tears then, flushed by this closeness, this mutual confession of fear and doubt, and I didn't know whether she was going to hell or not. Worse than that, it was just possible that when I said "No you're not," I might've been lying right then, maybe even blaspheming the holy spirit my own self. How could you know?

* * *

And so we sat in a yellow oaken pew in the back row where I liked to rest my hand on her knee, far from parents' prying eyes. Just the touch of shimmering cinnamon nylons could set me trembling, but tonight there would be no furtive caressing, as we gazed up from a packed pew into laser eyes of the world's foremost expert on hell. That's what the fliers called him. He'd studied the scriptures for a book and for a 33-rpm recording about hell that he would offer for sale after the service. And he'd studied about it for a permanent educational exhibition hall he was building in Gatlinburg with the help of the Lord. More to the point, God had called him to make hell real for everyone within the sound of his voice. And so he did. Standing there before us, he began his sermon smooth as the man on the FM radio.

"Those roads are awful slick tonight, brothers and sisters, what with the rain that's begun to fall, bringing oils oozing to the surface of the pavement. Imagine if you were to die in a car wreck before you made it home tonight?" He took off his yellow jacket with the broken black stripes, and loosened his narrow red tie. Then he rolled up his sleeves and his baritone took on a southern twang.

"Now if you should die in a state of sin unredeemed by the blood of Christ you'd immediately find yourself in hell. Some say you stand before a throne to be judged, but if that's so, it happens in the twinkling of an eye. I've personally watched sinners go down to eternity complaining of the heat with their last breath. I've heard them squall and cry out that flames were licking their toes. So, dear sinner, don't think there's a break between the dying and the waking up in hell for there is none. One second you are on your deathbed and the next you're lost in the agony of hell fire that burns your flesh without devouring it, for the flesh of that eternal body we inhabit beyond the grave is made of materials that fire can never consume. NASA can create such materials, so believe me when I tell you, so can God, so can God, so can God. And thus you burn in agony of hell fire. Think of times you've scorched a finger on a matchstick or seared the flesh of your inner arm on the edge of an iron or scalded your tongue with coffee. Oh, there's no greater pain than burning. Now magnify such wounds a million times, because in the hereafter your entire body is a thousand times more sensitive than the tender-most flesh of your earthly body. And the liquid fires of hell, well, they're a thousand times hotter. So do the math. Scientists tell us of fires in volcanoes and on the planet Venus that wash to and fro like oceans of napalm and you're thrashing about in such fire, and sulfurous smoke burns into your nostrils and sinuses with each breath and you cannot turn away, though you turn and turn and turn."

A sudden spasm seized his neck and shoulders, rolled down both arms, fled his fingertips into the amen-pews and thence rolled through the congregation, row upon row clear back to us. It was then his voice developed a sort of hitch common to many a Smoky Mountain preacher in which every expressed thought is punctuated with a shouted syllable, "hah!"

"And the waves wash against the cavern walls of hell, *hah*, and splash into a thousand drops, *hah*, and rebound across your flesh, *hah*, burning you clear to the bone!" Then he whispered in a voice that was awful to hear. "But those bones and those muscles and those nerves never burn up they just *buuurrrrn*." Now he was shouting again. "And your head stee-e-eams with black curling smoke as fingers of fire wash through roots of your hair and fill up all the caverns of Hades, and in the light cast by a billion flames you behold arms reaching up from the lake of fire and here and there the arms and faces of loved ones who never took Jesus into their hearts rise from liquid waves and they grab at their eyes with phosphorous hands and pluck those very eyeballs out of their heads and fling them away like glowing cinders, *hah*, as they cry out to you, *hah*, screaming and pleading for you to DO SOMETHING! but those eyes grow back again and again and never can be closed.

"Oh for one drop of cold water to touch against my poor parched tongue, voices cry out as the rich man cried, 'Father Abraham, have mercy on me, and send Lazarus that he may dip the tip of his finger in water and cool my tongue, for I am tormented in this flame.' Did I say *parched tongue* a moment ago? I meant to say *broiling, swollen* tongue. I meant to say *writhing* and *thrashing* around inside your own oven mouth *tongue*.

"And your eyes blaze and blaze but never go blind because the devil wants you to see what you've done to yourself, *hah*. Wants you to live it, *hah*. Wants you to remember the sins of your life, *hah*, and all the opportunities that passed you by, *hah*, times like tonight, *hah*, when you could've come up this aisle and given your hearts over to... *Jesus...*" he whispered the name.

Kelly Sue's hands clenched mine until I lost feeling there as Hamby began naming hell-bound souls—including Jezebel, Delilah, Pontius Pilate, Nebukanezzar, King Herod, Judas and then Stalin and Hitler and Jayne Mansfield and Elvis—if he didn't change his ways—and even Perry Jenkins—who'd killed his girlfriend over in Knoxville the week before—so that we all tensed in fear he'd name one of us. And with tension clutching us, he begged us to be saved.

A score at least walked or ran crying down that aisle, including Kelly and me, who rededicated our lives, but if that round of salvation took hold you'd never know it from her mournful face next time we met beneath our bent tree in the gullies. Still, I knew right off she'd changed. She didn't offer sweet lips and neck for kissing, neither did she stretch and lie down to be spooned, and for a time she stopped coming to the gullies altogether. At night, in my desire for her I burned like a planet sucked in too close to some blazing star, and amid the all too real flames of my imagined hell I said Lord just send me on down if that's the price of loving Kelly Sue.

* * *

It was an early Saturday about two months later that our sturdy black phone rang in the living room and my father picked it up, said hello, then "How's it going, Rev. Hamby?" After they talked he sat studying on something, his wide gray eyes looking to some middle distance. Slowly they relaxed, panning round until they rested on my face at the doorway.

"Lonnie, let's go to Gatlinburg. Looks like Hell's about to open for business."

"Well, the thing is Daddy," I swallowed hard, "I was supposed to go over to Kelly's to uh..."

"That's off for now son, you both need to see this. Get her on the phone."

It was a hot afternoon by the time we got to "A Tour Through Hell," its letters blazing Gothic and blood-drenched on a fiery sign. The building was about twice the size of a revival tent and had three peaks painted in lava red over ash-black shingles. It looked out of place amid all the tourist shops—Taffy Town, House of Mirrors, Rebel Corner. Evidently tourists weren't all that interested in touring hell during vacation, for we were the only ones in the new-paved parking lot as we got out of Daddy's Buick, save for a bored woman selling soft drinks from a painted plywood booth. More blazing letters—cherry red, lemon yellow, announced, "Snow Cones from Hell." We stood looking at those words.

"Preacher Hamby!" Daddy's voice called, interrupting our reveries.

We turned to behold a brown and pink creature with at least two dozen arms but just two legs ambling across the pavement. We saw that it was Rev. Hamby carrying an unwieldy pile of mannequin arms—elbows and bent fingers pointing all around in the sunshine. Sweat dripped from his blond-white hair, and it took him a few seconds to get a good look at who was addressing him. When he did, he set down his load, which clattered like dice as he pulled out a handkerchief. Laser eyes scanned us, lingered over Kelly's calves, knees, her blossoming bosom and fair colorations of her face so like his own. He cleared his throat, nodded at us, stepped around the pile of mannequin limbs and shook my daddy's hand. They exchanged pleasantries, then the preacher asked if we'd help carry the arms inside and we said sure. He ushered us to the Gates of Hell, where Daddy offered to pay, but he waved it off.

"Just tell others," he said as we entered the warm breath of a man-made cavern. He led us down labyrinthine halls bordered by black and red stalagmites and stalactites of spray-painted foam marking entrances to side-caverns where denizens hid amid shadows. Carefully, Kelly Sue and I balanced our phony arms.

When we came to a side-opening larger than most, Rev. Hamby began taking hold of them and, holding each vertically, hands-aloft, worked one after another into pre-cut slots in the black and red floor, molded to resemble lava. After he'd positioned all the arms, he reached around a black pillar, flipped a switch and we heard a fan whir into motion, blowing paper flames up to flicker amid red and orange lights so that a sea of arms appeared to rise from a fluttery hell for lost mannequins.

Rev. Hamby smiled, "I'm adding a few heads tomorrow," and we smiled back, for he was charming, despite the sweat and the menial task at hand. We were beguiled by more than his charm, though we couldn't have told you what.

"Now we can start over," he said as he led us out beneath a No Exit sign into bright sunshine and again to the Gates of Hell.

Tortured screams resumed as black lights marked a labyrinthine path, and now electric candlesticks flared as we approached raven-haired Delilah, lofting huge shears to gaze at us between silvery blades. Wiggy ropes of Samson's hair trailed from her left hand beside an exposed thigh extending from a slit in her dark and sparkly skirt. Tinny speakers hidden amid molten foam recited pertinent scripture in Hamby's voice. Nearby was Judas with bulging eyes. Frozen dark fingers clutched at a noose around his neck as his other hand lofted an empty pouch. In a cloud about his swarthy head, thirty gold coins dangled from fishing line.

Cain, Herod, Jezebel, Jayne Mansfield were all there for us to gawk at in turn, each less real than the previous until, both of us yawning, Kelly Sue and I looked blankly at the Lake of Fire again with its mannequin arms. As we stepped out beneath the confusing No Exit exit-sign and into bright daylight, Daddy patted his face with a handkerchief, coughed once and, looking past Hamby, said, "That was really something." The evangelist took him by a fleshy upper arm, leaned into him and spoke earnestly in hopeful tones as Kelly and I craned our necks to look up and down the streets of Gatlinburg.

"It's hot as blazes out here," we heard Hamby say at last. Looking at us he rolled his lips together. "Constance," he called, "give these children snow cones."

We skipped over to the plywood booth where the tired woman scooped crushed ice from coolers beneath the counter and mounded it atop flimsy paper cones, then pumped syrup from a rainbow array of jugs. She smiled as she handed us the cones and we stood on the pavement making eyes at one another and eating Snow Cones from Hell. They tasted just like any snow cones we'd ever slurped at a Gatlinburg tourist dive.

"Children!" Daddy yelled across the lot, and we drifted over to him. "I hope this has... taught you a... thing or two...." His voice trailed off as he fished for his keys. He knew as well as we did that *A Tour Through Hell* was doomed to fail, that it had cheapened a cherished and terrible tenet of our faith. He herded us to the car as he tossed goodbyes over his shoulder at Rev. Hamby.

He stood there looking strangely forsaken as we drove off.

I don't remember anything else from that day save for the scent of cedar and red clay earth and the smile that played about Kelly Sue's lips moments after she murmured, "I'm tired, Lonnie, I'm going to sleep now. Spoon me if you'd care to." And as dusk settled in, the heat of early summer bathed two mortal bodies with more of heaven than we would ever know, or ever care to know.

At the Körperwelten Exhibit, Köln Germany

Janée J. Baugher

"Those attending this exhibition can obtain unique insights into healthy and un-healthy bodies.... More than 200 authentic plastinated human specimens can be seen, including whole-bodies as well as individual organs and transparent body slices. Thanks to the process of plastination, which has been invented and developed by Gunther von Hagens, the fluids in human tissue is [sic] replaced with special plastics.... The specimens are dry and odourless and have a rigidity that allows completely new types of artistic display."
(from the exhibit pamphlet)

The English pamphlet reads "Anatomy Art."
My interpreter says "Body World."

I. BRACKETS

The superficial muscles have been pried off and discarded
to reveal his myriad of nerves—flat iridescent lengths.
    Metallic of fascia, ligament, tendon.
    How to differentiate between the pearl-yellow
of tendons and ligaments with the egg-grey of nerve?
He sits at the table; both forearms rest lightly on the platform.
    The unveiled conduit from cerebellum—
    its offspring splaying out, interweaving through
the vertebrae. Before him, a chess board. The top of his
skull was removed, its intact brain remains there—stealth in
    grey matter. The spinal cord's vast matrix
    emanating out to its purpose, that translation

of idea to action. Anatomical language. The black bishop
waits in his hand. Yet the artistic brain grows myopic at the sight
    of chess. Hence, this prop versus
    a canvas to which his plastinated hand
steadies the brush. Yes, proceed, thin nexus man,
you're so close to apprehending that queen.

II. HYPHEN

The upright man is
doffed of skin where
areas on the body are
slid forward like drawers

        (two on his torso, one
        on his arm, two on
        the leg). In other areas:
        flaps open out on the

                vertical like cabinets
                (one reveals the hip
                joint; one, the intestines;
                and one, the heart).

Even the face protrudes
like a box that can be
pushed back into place.
A human body which

        mimics a bureau, a cup-
        board—drawers and doors
        securing the owner's anti-
        quities: some sequestered,

some quite notorious—steel
vaults and revolving doors.
Portals others can enter—those
we cannot cross ourselves.

On some days the
do-not-disturb sign
hangs on our handles
like a cowl of thistle.

III. SOLIDUS

He stands in three pulled-apart parts: three torsos, three arms, three legs.
His center of gravity is lowered over his front, semi-bent knee. All arms
meet at the handle of a fencing foil. He brandishes it out at us in an *en
garde.*

His left portion retains most of the body's superficial anterior muscles.
The long-rope muscles of the sartorius and gracilius juxtapose his sulky
three-part sex. The face consists of all facial fibers plus the top cranium.

His middle section includes deep back muscles, the internal organs and
the cerebellum situated inside the posterior cranium. The right portion
owns all the body's superficial posterior muscles. At the pinnacle: the lone
cerebrum.

Denuded and parted, he keeps us at bay and thinks: look how smug you
are, so invincible in your vestured organ. You, ignorant to how muscles
weep, how the brain processes, how adrenaline tastes. Oblivious of the
plexus of nerve and blood,

and how they stay their course. Blind to synaptic entropy, the tone of
nerves reacting to fear. Force to force, body to body—this metaphysical
system and that insular, inconsequential soul.

IV. DASH

In a fixed position the man runs.
      The groups of muscle
            tenuously peel away
               and trail behind him,
                    each scarcely attached to bone.

The near-skeleton
      (with trusses of brawn caught, as if in a wind tunnel)
          flees as if he's distancing himself
            from musculature,
               attempting to escape its meaning.

An exodus from gender,
      that construct under which men are placed:
          regarded by physical prowess.
            To quit the fibrous,
               physiology of meat-to-bone,
                  the hormone of Y.

But will running free him—
      all ocean and land,
          coördinates under skin?

V. PARENTHESES

Although he's split in two lengthwise, even his wife
would recognize his droopy earlobes and crew cut.

The halves hang side by side. His strong,
defeated arms and aged, smudged tattoo. Under

each fingernail, a welter of dirt. She would tell you
it's because of the horses. Every other summer weekend

they would show them. He preferred stock seat equitation,
and she, dressage. He'd kiss her the same whether she took

the purple or the blue—the man whom she mourns tonight
feeding their thoroughbreds the hay he baled.

VI. QUESTION MARK

The confidence
of her stance—corrugated tissue,
the byway of live-shade sinew, the tread
of tendon, abutment of bone. Although the blanket
of skin was lost, two sharp nipples and areolas were preserved—
thoughtfully dissected and pinned back onto two mounds of plastinated
adipose. Abdomen's sliced down the middle to expose organs pushed north
for placenta and five-month fetus—fetal-pink against listless grey. Balancing
upside-down, curled like a napping cat. The lip of the woman's clitoris—
quite wilted—drooping five brown hairs. The dead baby
inside her still: no birthdays, no cakes—chocolate
with white frosting and candles, the way they
smoke lightly in thin wires just
after they're blown
out.

VII. EXCLAMATION POINT

In one room, a circular tiered display: on black velour, dead human babies.
Buddha-figures rotating clockwise. Some afflicted with disease, some just pre-
formed. So many questions. Fingers pointing, no one says a word. No divider

between us and them. If one rolled off, surely there'd be pairs of hands to catch it. We emerge from this room as from a mosque, and into the next: a display of embryos suspended in large glass cylinders lined in a row on a table. Behind the table, a father tries to sooth his bawling newborn.

VIII. PERIOD

I squat in front of an   upright human corpse.
His muscle fibers retain   their rose.
The staunch fascia,   taut on the abdomen.
At this vantage,   his inoffensive penis
and two testes   dangling on thick cords.
Gathered on his   right arm, the extent
of his hollow skin   The back and headdress,
sheets of pink,   but the flesh of arms
seems slinked out of.   The foot skin
hangs down like a tossed   slipper.
He faces toward the   skin-drape in worship.
And, seeing how   easy it is to become separated,
divided into   parts, the dead and the living,
the blood   inside my own body escapes.

❋
The Turtle's Leash
Emily Dziuban

Eleven hours in the car got us from New Jersey to South Carolina, a state, my friends had assured me, where people actually flew the rebel flag and married their cousins at church with the preacher's blessing. I had a grandmother it was time I met, my mother said. I slept most of the ride down, which is what I do when I'm nervous, though I tell my mother I'm just tired.

When I woke, the car was still, off not idling, and my mother was gone. We were here. I looked around and saw three trailers decreasing in size like nesting dolls, a double-wide, a single-wide, and a camper. A satellite dish, round as a hot tub, was pole-mounted in the middle of the sandy yard. I got out of the car and looked around. I couldn't see another house or a paved road. Our car was parked closest to the camper, so I walked up a set of unattached, wooden steps and opened the door.

"There's our girl," Mom said in a voice that was too glad to see me. She bugged her eyes at me, head-nodded toward my grandmother. I stalled on introducing myself by scanning the room, literally one room. A bed against one wall, a stove against another and two chairs in the middle.

When my eyes got to my grandmother, I freaked a bit more than I should have. She reached her arms out, but I pulled back like a toddler, not like a high-schooler who knows better.

My grandmother was receding into herself like she meant to get smaller to fit her house better. Her osteoporotic back, curved liked a question mark, kept her head from bumping the low roof. I couldn't see lips, only skin curled over teeth and gums. The lips had pulled back into their own mouth like they meant to touch the inside of the skull that held them. I couldn't even pretend to be willing to kiss that mouth.

"She's scared," my grandmother said.

"She's tired," Mom said.

"Yeah, I'm tired. Sorry." I sat in the only open chair, leaving my grandmother nowhere to sit.

"Long drive to country relatives," my grandmother said.

We were to stay in the single-wide because I had an aunt and two cousins living in the double. Mom let me drive the car from in front of the camper to in front of the single. I carried our bags inside but couldn't bring myself to put them in the bedrooms or go back to the camper. I sat down on top of the bags and listened to the trailer make sounds. I could hear wind, not just against the windows but against the walls. Occasional scratching sounds came from beneath the floor like small animals were nesting in the underpinning. My footsteps on any part of the floor sounded on every part of the floor. After what had to be an hour, I heard someone approaching.

"You stuck up?" a boy's voice said through the door. He didn't have to open the door to be heard.

"No," I said, not moving.

"Come on, then. Let's get to the woods."

The older cousin was Jimmy. The younger was Corneal, but just call him Scooter, Jimmy said. They gave me an open can of soda called Cheerwine. They had obviously been drinking from it because red syrup caked the corners of their mouths giving them clowns' smiles. Back at school, when new guys came, my girls and I did what we called taking a temperature. We checked a few things to gauge how hot or cold the guy was. We checked nails (trim and no engine dust), split ends (none), shoes (clean), corners of the eyes (attended to), and hands (moisturized, not cut up). My cousins would have scaled worse than grease monkeys. They were dirt monkeys, the kind of boys who were too busy being boys to take a bath.

Jimmy and Scooter negotiated the woods like they were born in it. Tree branches clawed at me with every step, but I refused to squeal like spoiled city girl. They led me around for a long time, often claiming a creek was just ahead, but they probably just wanted to test me.

We found the turtle before noon. It was big as a dinner plate, but the cousins didn't hesitate to pick it up. "You shouldn't do that," I said, "It could have rabies."

"These things don't get rabies," Jimmy said. "Only bats and mammals."

I stared at him for knowing the word mammals. Then the turtle peed, a yellow stream that fell long and loud between it and the ground. Scooter laughed, and though I could feel a few drops hitting the toes of my canvas sneakers, I laughed too. It had never occurred to me that turtles would pee.

"Let's take it to maw maw," Jimmy said.

Maw maw, as Jimmy called my grandmother, was frying something. When Scooter opened the door, the burnt-grease smell flowed out and covered me like un-dammed water. I could almost feel it soaking through my cloths and hair and skin. I might have retched, but the cousins weren't reacting to the smell. They charged right in, Jimmy straight-arming the turtle out from his body. Mom sat on her same chair reading, which I didn't take to be a good sign. She and her own mother had already finished talking after not seeing each other (I thought) for fifteen years.

"Lookit," Jimmy said loudly, eyes fixed on his prize.

"You mean to throw it in the pot?" my grandmother said. She didn't turn, perhaps because it would have taken her a long time. This was the closest I'd stood to her since we got here. Her back fascinated me. It was hard to believe she couldn't just straighten up. When Mom told me to straighten up, I could. If we set the turtle on her back, it wouldn't fall off, like setting it on a table.

"Hell, no. We mean to keep it."

"Keep it outside then. Dinner'll be ready shortly."

I looked at my mother. She mouthed "lunch" back at me.

Outside, we examined the turtle as good as any veterinarian could. I knew because I thought about going pre-vet in college, but I'd never been this close to anything other than a dog or cat or fish or hamster. The turtle had pulled every appendage it could into its shell when we picked it up, so we looked at the head and legs from the side. Its underside was yellowish and smooth, like a rock touched by a lot of people. All three of us stroked the top of the shell, dark and lumpy, as if the turtle could feel our petting. I kept my hand on the turtle's back even though Jimmy and Scooter's fingers sometimes brushed mine.

"Let's name it," I said.

"Scooter," Scooter said. His first word that day.

Mom came to the door and called us in. "Leave the animal outside," she said.

"We can't. He'll run away," I said.

"It's a turtle, honey. They barely move. Use your reasoning skills." Mom's stress showed in the tone of her voice. This visit wasn't going well, and I should have been easier on her, but I didn't want to leave the turtle. I brushed past her into the grease-clouded camper. The cousins followed me like allies.

We ate chicken from styrofoam plates, kids cross-legged on the floor, mom sitting in a chair, grandmother folded in a chair. The cousins and I kept cutting looks at each other. When we were close to done, my grandmother said, "Y'all get a critter and feel like kin now." I didn't like that. I'd slipped into thinking that these people were regular, and she saw it.

We had left the turtle by the wooden steps, but it was gone when we got out.

"Spread out," Jimmy said.

We combed the yard, Scooter yelling "Scooter" as if the turtle would answer.

I found it, proof enough that the turtle preferred me. "Here," I yelled. I picked it up while it retracted its legs and head back under its shell. My grandmother had come out onto her wooden steps and stood smoking a pipe.

"Bring it here," she said, louder than I would have guessed she could. I brought her the turtle. She sat on the step, pre-bent over, and held the turtle between the insteps of her feet. She reached into the front pocket of her dress, and for a moment I was too distracted by the thought of a dress with pockets to realize what she brought out. The object was a screwdriver. She put the pointy end against the turtle's shell and started to twist. I screamed. I screamed with enough something's-really-wrong to bring my mother outside. Flecks of the turtle's shell collected like sawdust.

"What's going on?" Mom said.

"Kids are playing with a critter. Kids are acting like kids," my grandmother said.

Mom leaned far over to get a look, then said, real casual-like, "You leashing the turtle?"

"You want anything you love to stay near you, you got to tied it up or pen it. I can tell you that."

I watched horrified, certain that she meant to kill it and put it in her fry-pot. She screwed two holes near its neck, one on each side. The turtle didn't make a sound or bleed. It just stayed retracted. Jimmy smiled through the whole procedure and kept looking at me to make the point that see, I was, in fact, spoiled. When she told him to, Jimmy "fetched" her a string. My grandmother threaded the string through the two holes, tied off the end, and handed it me, making a shape with her imploded mouth that could or could not have been a smile.

"How'd you do that?" I asked, even though I had watched from start to finish.

"Shell's only connected to the body at certain points. You can cut some parts of the shell without cutting the animal. Now it can't get away from you."

We tied the turtle to a tree and set a bowl of water and some lettuce near it, but it refused to take either. Later that afternoon, Jimmy and Scooter got bored and went back to the woods and to not taking baths. Mom, I pretty sure, read a novel a day sitting in that chair. I stayed with the turtle. By the end of the third day, it was dead at the end of its string. Though I would never say so, killing the turtle was totally worth it so I could spend the weekend checking on it and stroking its feet when it got too tired to hold them in anymore.

THE INFLUENCE OF SKIN

Sara Roberts

I will trade blackened tuna fillet for lemon Jell-O,
original for diet, extra caffeine,
Reese's peanut butter cups for Ephedra.

I will make you drool.

You will ogle my bones
and know
    consumed by a hunger
    greater than mine
that you fucked up.

You will fantasize lapping fruit and cream
from the porcelain bowl
of my hollow pelvic bone

as I lie flat-backed,
whipped dollops
punctuating
my strawberry skin
    your Kleenex thrusts.

Cleanup will be slow, gooey.

My empty bones
will be worth
every
ounce.

MOON SEEING

Susan Deer Cloud

After you left, I no longer could sleep on our garret bed.
Instead, I slept on the old bed you dragged
into the living room—
we were too poor to buy a couch. Tonight I felt brave,
climbed the stairs to where we once held each other
against the night. When my marriage broke up
I nailed a card to bare wall: "Barn's burnt down,
now I can see the moon." My affair with you done
I re-read Masahide's words, slip
between burgundy sheets, satin
celestial fingers on my skin.

A quarter century ago I read how George Sand
wanted to be with just one man. Her wish turned into
many lovers. So she ooh la la'd, "Each lover
is a new education for me." Even then I suspected
my fate might be French. I couldn't keep away
from French films. Nights I dreamed in the language
and Jean Paul Belmondo licked me breathless
the way you did on our garret bed decades later—
your Asian mouth thicker than Jean's, your eyes
languorous eagles.

I stretch my flesh on the satins of memory
the way my Persian cat stretches hers.
January moon spills light through window.

Moon Seeing

My winter hair spills across your ghost
and his come-cries floating out into outer space forever.
I close eyes—smile. Have I not
grown more educated?

KIDS IN SAVANNAH PARK
Richard Remine

Auto Body

Bob Thompson

Your neck and shoulders are stiff as steel
from year after year of day after day
of driving in traffic,
driving in traffic,
driving in tragic
traffic.
Brake lights in your eyes,
one hand clutching the wheel, one halfway between fist
and prayer—
merciful God please just vaporize that idiot!!! Buick trying
to turn left.
Sitting
sitting
sitting
in traffic.
Everything's congested:
blood pressure warning light flash on the dash
brain overflowing with roadside trash
exhaust fumes trapped in your throat
asphalt up your ass
18-wheelers crowding in
McDonald's arches kinking your spine.
You desperately need realigned.

Bob Thompson

Listen to
your
poor
overheated
six cylinder
heart.

Fat Girls

Ellen Dennis Stein

I AM A fat girl and my girl is a fat girl and my grandmother told my father to be sure to dance with the fat girls she was a fat girl herself and I bet my father did and I dance with a fat girl every chance I get and my cousin Gertrude was a fat girl and I know that fat girls have more brains my mother's mother was a Morehead and she was just plump and not as bright as my Dad's mother who was fat and my mother was tall taller than my father and she was thin and she always said just lose an extra five pounds so you've got some leeway or was it lee weigh? and she had no idea what that five pounds cost in denial and I never did lose that five pounds and I was always terrified that I would be fat because my mother was not but she called herself scrawny chicken-necked so why did she want me to be thin and it doesn't matter anyway because I am who I am and I'm smart and all the fat girls who dance are smart and the ones who sit out should be smart enough to know to get up and dance with each other all those brains on the dance floor and all those delicious curves and soft breasts give me a fat girl any day because I am a fat girl and the girl I married is a fat girl and we dance so well together you should see us.

BORDER TOWN SCHOOL

Katie O'Sullivan

Barefoot
I left my shoes at home,
Played with my classmates,
Where our dusty foot prints
were all the same
Color.

Nice Day

Kali Meister

She was sitting at work when it occurred to her that it
    might be a good idea
for her to scream. She felt the power—power of the
    voice rumbling
through the soul that was silenced by the body.

She thought it might be time to set her voice free.

She ponders what could happen if her body gave birth to
    the sound that broke glass,
shook the earth and cleanses the mind completely of the
    pound, pound, pound
against her body.

His body was heavy, wet with perspiration and permeated
    the air
with the odor of Crown Royal and Pierre Carden—a smell
    that, when the body
is angry or agitated, the soul will remember.

It developed in the chest, beneath his weight, his smell,
and his sticky, sticky lies. Beneath his fingers—his eyes, his
    mouth,
his skin, his eyes, his mouth, his skin and the sound of his
    heart beating
that still turns her inside out.

Yet her voice chooses to abstain. The scream declines,
    tucked safe
inside, the soul and the heart. They are safe inside her,
    the woman
with home and job and boys, boys, boys.

Still, there is no scream. She wants to scream for the
    fathers who lie.
She wants to scream for a mother's denial. But most of all
she wants to scream because it hurts to hold the
    voice inside
for twenty years, to fight the anger, to play the strong,
    to forget
and then remember.

It would be a good day to get into the car and drive,
windows down, wind spirals around her. She is ready,
wanting to let go, let go. She is ready to recall the sound
of the room where her soul lost the battle with his body,
where his body overpowered her body. She is ready
to recall the place where the walls echo the story—
    the story
of the scream and its conception. She is ready for the story
of the car that rattles to the country where it will be time
for her to scream.

My mother refuses mastectomy, winter 2005

William Orem

She still believes in Christ; the old sure type,
gives coins to saints to find her wandered keys.
As a child I'd watch those copper faces peering
from beneath the marble feet of Anthony,

his sandaled stone. This season by some chance
the winter sparrows left their berry shreds
in red striations on the whitened land.
It makes one think of blood—divine, or men's—

one never fully leaves the Catholic dream.
A field of blood on winter snow. A cup;
a cup of bleeding from the whitest fleece.
The hope of worlds beyond this frozen one,

the ancient praise of holy suffering.
Alone, the earth dreams of its blossoming.

SACRED

Melanie Williams

Swiss researchers have discovered
that human tears are dripping
with serotonin.
It explains the calm
after the storm.
There's that fullness—
proof our grief is potent,
more than just salt.

But haven't we known it
forever?

Ancient Hebrews
collected their tears
in porcelain cups, guarding them
like jewels, treasure.
Those who had suffered
were esteemed.

When the crops failed and
the children were hungry,
their empty bellies protruding
into the dust,

when mothers lost their
sons, when sons became cruel, when
the red heat seared across
sweating shoulders, when all
that was left for hope
was the uncertainty of leaving,

the cups overflowed.

UNTITLED (DETAIL)
Karley J. Sullivan

✳

SINGING THE BODY ELECTRIC
Jeanne McDonald

RICHARD STANDS IN the kitchen, shifting from one bare foot to the other. He's wearing the flannel pajamas I gave him for Christmas. Blue plaid. Bottoms only. His dark hair springs out in a dozen different directions. He's crying. Jesus, he's *crying*. And he tells me again, as if I hadn't heard the first time: "Leah used to be my *wife*. Who else is going to take care of her?"

I tell him nobody wants to take care of her, can't he remember all the reasons why he left her? But he says this is different because she's dying, and she's all alone. She has a month, maybe less.

My God, the people we know don't die. How old is Leah? Twenty-four?

Richard shifts his stance again and his pajama bottoms slip down on his skinny hips, exposing his navel and the dark hair that swirls up under the elastic band. I love his flat stomach, his lean, hard body, but he's not thinking about how I feel. He blows his nose with a dirty sock from the laundry basket.

"She doesn't want strangers in the house." Right, I tell myself. She doesn't want just anybody seeing her wasted body, wiping her bottom, cleaning up her vomit. She wants the ex-husband. He's *seen* the body in better times, he's loved it, kissed it, slept with it. So yeah, use him and get even with the new wife, who happens to be me.

I decide to ask practical questions, stay away from the emotional. "But how can you take care of her and finish your dissertation?"

Richard rolls his eyes. Oh, this is so Richard. The pregnant pause. He *enunciates*, pushing out his lips. "I've got this *sabbatical*," he says. "Re-

member? A semester off from teaching. I'll just work at her place. She's on morphine now. She sleeps a lot." He bangs his forehead against the wall. "Joanie, Joanie, this is not about sex, this is about somebody dying, for Chrissake." Mad now. Pissed off. Turning it all back on me. Okay, truth is, I just don't *care* if she's dying. Here I am, married six months and now my husband's going to stay with his ex for a month? "This is a no-brainer, Joanie," says Richard. "I *have* to do this."

"Over my dead body," I say. This is a good line, an ironic line, and I start laughing, can't stop. I'm hysterical, half crying, half howling. Jesus, *I'm* the wife now, *I'm* the wife.

"Try to understand, Joanie," he says, "will you just frigging try?" He bares his teeth, I swear it. Who does that? What civilized person bares his teeth in this millennium? "It's for a month, maybe, *a month,* Joanie. Can't you give her *that* long because then she'll be *dead.* Amen. No more late night phone calls, no more keying your car or slashing your tires. No more nasty letters. A month and you can have your comfortable little life back, everything neat and simple."

God, I can't believe his sarcasm, not over *this* huge an event. I rush into the bedroom, start scooping his clothes out of drawers, raking the hangers across the rod in his closet and tossing out jackets and pants. I want fireworks, I want drama, but the soft clothing doesn't make enough noise. So I grab the lamp on the bedside table, slam it against the door. That works. It shatters—that beautiful old green library lamp Richard's had since graduate school. "Get out," I scream. "Go to her, comfort her with apples, morphine, whatever. Sleep with her. But don't expect to find me here when you get back." My heart's pounding. I'm not mad anymore, just scared he might do what I tell him to.

"Be reasonable," he says about this unreasonable issue. "Nobody sleeps with a dying woman. And it won't be for that long. A couple of months at most."

Oh, so now it's a *couple* of months. Doesn't Richard remember how she lied, how she slept with other men, how she maxed out his credit cards? Has he forgotten we're still making payments on that little red convertible she bought on his credit? Wait a minute. Maybe there's hope. What about her parents?

"They're," he hesitates, "estranged. Something about her getting their retirement savings out of their bank account." He points a finger at me. "And I'm ahead of you on *this* one: She can't *afford* a nursing home, and she wouldn't go if she could." His cell phone rings. He grabs it up from the bedside table and paces as he listens. "Okay," he says. "Calm down, sweetie."

Sweetie?

"Stop crying. I'll be there." He glances at me and hangs up. "She's fallen," he says. "Can't make it back to bed. She's on the bathroom floor." He waves his hand to deter my protest of how she made the call. "She always carries the cell phone in the pocket of her bathrobe, just in case." He presses his palms together, prayerlike. "I have to go, Joanie," he says. "I *have* to."

I position myself in the doorway, blocking his exit. "Richard, we'll get her a nurse. I'll pay for it. I'll get a second job."

"Let me by, Joanie. I have to go." Then he realizes he's not dressed, and he's rummaging through the shirts I've thrown to the floor, picks one, pulls it on and in his haste buttons it crookedly so that one side is longer than the other. "I'm going now, okay?" He's still wearing the pajama bottoms. He's barefooted. "Let me by," he says again.

"No." I leap toward him, screaming, and shards of the broken lamp pierce my foot and I collapse against the wall. He sidesteps the whole crumpled mess I've morphed into and heads toward the door. It's too dangerous in this room for him even to pick up his moccasins. When I hear him drive away I crawl to the bed, wrap the white sheet around my bleeding foot, and cover my head with the quilt. If Richard comes home to discover that I have bled to death, he'll be sorry.

Or not.

I wake up with my foot throbbing, the bedclothes soaked with blood. It's dark outside, and my head pounds every time my heart beats. I turn on the surviving bedside lamp and look at the clock. It's ten past nine. I decide to call Richard to tell him I'm bleeding to death, but while I'm dialing I see that he left his cell phone on the floor when he was putting the crooked shirt on. I'll call *her*, then. Leah. *Leah* Sanders. She's kept her married name, Richard's name. I know where she lives—Maynard

Avenue—because Richard pointed out the house to me one day. The only time I'd seen Leah, though, was shortly after our wedding, in a restaurant. She was thin and very tall, with shiny black hair that fell to her waist, and she was beautiful in the way certain Jewish women are beautiful, dark-skinned and exotic, her nose prominent but somehow majestic. I remember thinking that an uncommon face is much more dangerous competition than a conventionally beautiful one, because that meant she had something else that attracted Richard. Drama, sexuality, a body compelling and electric.

That night at the restaurant she tiptoed up behind Richard and put her hands over his eyes, and I noticed she was still wearing her wedding ring. When she leaned forward, her hair spilled over her shoulders like folded silk. When she said *Guess who?* Richard laughed and said, *Leah*.

Now I remember that she's not listed in the phone book, has only a cell phone. And if I drive over there, Richard will hate me. I limp around the room, rip the bloody sheets from the bed, sweep up the broken glass. I can't stop crying and I can't sleep, so at midnight I decide to go to Leah's anyway—who cares what they think. My foot is still bleeding and so swollen that I have to wear Richard's moccasins, one of which seems to be filling up with blood.

The ride is hell because I have to use my cut foot on the clutch whenever I shift gears, so I just leave the car in second and drift through stop signs and red lights. When I finally get there, the house is dark except for a small lamp by the living room window. I park behind the sports car bought with Richard's credit card, hobble up the front steps, and for a few minutes I just listen. Nothing. I knock softly. There's a noise from deep inside the house, and finally Richard's at the door, squinting against the porch light he's turned on. He's still wearing the crooked shirt, and his pajama pants have some sort of yellow stain on the leg. When he sees me staring at it, his jaw tightens. "She threw up on me."

I gather all my strength to keep from crying. "I want you home."

Leah is calling from the bedroom. "Baby? Baby, who's there?"

Richard is slowly pulling the door closed. "She can't even get to the bathroom alone."

I think about pushing my foot in the door, but the sticky dampness in

Richard's shoe stops me. "Hire a nurse to take care of her," I hiss. "Hire a goddamned nurse."

"Joanie..."

I'm in so much pain and confusion, I don't have the strength to argue anymore. As I stumble down the steps Richard calls out. "Your foot. Oh my God, Joanie, you're bleeding."

As if I don't know this?

"You need to go to the emergency room, I mean it, Joanie. Right now." He hesitates and then says, "Hey, are those my shoes?"

I laugh. My foot is pulsating and a dark pool of blood seeps out around the heel of the moccasin and onto the broken concrete step. I feel faint and nauseated, but my vague plan is to stand there until all the blood drains from my body, leaving a permanent stain to mark my protest and a fresh corpse for Richard to have to dispose of. "Will you drive me there?" I ask

Richard's mouth crumples. He opens his hands, imploring. This is the point where I give up. I turn around again, limp toward my car, a beat-up yellow Volkswagen with over three hundred thousand miles on the odometer. I start the engine, scream in pain as I depress the clutch, shove the gear into first, and then I slam into Leah's convertible. I jerk into reverse, back up and slam into it again, four, maybe five times, each shift accompanied by screams of pain. The neighbors' lights come on. Richard runs down the steps, slips on the blood, and falls. When I shift into reverse, he scrambles back up the steps, probably thinking I'm coming after *him* this time. I do give that scenario a brief assessment, but instead pull away from the curb. At the hospital, I park by the emergency entrance and hobble in, leaving a single line of bloody footprints. Because of the bleeding, the girl at the desk takes me back to an examining room ahead of all the other broken and bruised people who have been waiting there, maybe for hours. A nurse gently removes all the slivers from my foot with a long pair of silver tweezers, then asks me if I've had a tetanus shot lately. I can't remember. The doctor comes in and gives me a tetanus shot. He is young and handsome, with eyes so blue and liquid I want to wade right into them and drown. He keeps patting my shoulder and cooing in a deep, dreamy voice. "It's all right, it's all right." He's beautiful in his white coat and seems so godlike I want to confess all my sins to him. When I'm finally able to stop bawling and tell him my story, he listens with appropriate frowning and shaking of the head. Then he tells me to lie back on the gurney while he stitches up my foot. He is so tender and precise that when he bandages it, I feel like a Christmas present. "I'm giving you something for pain," he says in his soothing baritone, "and something for infection. Keep the dressing dry, and come back in ten days to get the stitches out." He hands me a couple of bottles of pills, and then a third—Xanax—saying, "And these are for heartache."

I refuse his offer of a wheelchair. I prefer to limp out on the heel of Richard's moccasin. At the door I turn back to look at him. "Are you married?" I ask.

He laughs and shrugs his shoulders. "Sorry," he says.

Outside I climb into my smashed and bloody car. There's a half-empty bottle of water on the floor, and I swig down two of the heartbreak pills and start for home, but near Maynard Avenue I suddenly swerve to the right and pull up at Leah's house. I'm beginning to feel a little sick now, but once more I scuttle up the steps and onto the porch. Through the living room window I see Richard, asleep on the couch, tangled up in a thick blue afghan with a knotted fringe. When I tap on the window, he sits up, rubs his eyes, then unwinds himself and comes to the door. I rush to speak before he does, and out comes something I hadn't meant to say. "I want to help."

He pulls me into his arms. "Joanie, Joanie," he whispers, "I do love you, I do. Don't you know that?" He looks at my foot, gets down on one knee, and kisses the bandage.

"I want to see Leah," I tell Richard. He stares at me for a second, then pulls my left arm around his neck so he can shoulder my weight, and, three-legged, we maneuver the dark hallway. When we pass the kitchen, the overripe stench of garbage hits me and I glimpse an enormous stack of dirty dishes on the sink. "I'll clean those up in the morning," I say.

The bedroom is permeated by the sickly-sweet odor of vomit, and in the dim reflection of a night light, I see Leah lying on the bed. She looks smaller than I remembered, and her hair is gone now, from the chemo. Her scalp gleams and her skin looks yellow. Her lips are cracked and dry.

I gasp without realizing it, and she opens her eyes. "Oh," she croaks. "It's you."

"I thought..." I begin. "I thought maybe I could help. But if you don't want me here..."

She closes her eyes and turns over. "Stay," she whispers. "Thank you."

Richard swoops me up in his arms and carries me back to the living room. Somehow we fit on the sofa together, and Richard falls asleep almost at once, but the heartache pills aren't working for me yet. I keep thinking about Leah in the restaurant that time, how her silky black hair had slid across her shoulders as she leaned over Richard's chair. She'd been wearing a slinky red dress and high-heeled red satin shoes with ankle straps. Now I keep picturing those shoes in the dark closet of her bedroom, standing empty, the dress hanging shapeless on a wire hanger.

Just as I'm dropping off to sleep, Leah calls from the back of the house. "It hurts so bad. Oh God somebody help me."

I ease out of his arms and limp down the dark hallway. On the bathroom windowsill I find the morphine, and on the sink, a cloudy glass that I fill with water. I help Leah sit up while she swallows the tablet, and then I climb into bed with her and hold her while she sobs. "It's all right, Leah," I whisper, staring into the dark. "It's all right. I'm here now. I'm here."

CUTTER

Clint Stivers

Many times
as a young girl,
she would:
crack free a razor blade
from its plastic Gillette sheath;
sift through the silverware drawer
for the best black handled knife;
or break the mouth of a Mason jar
for a curving shard.

But now
she slowly reaches for her X-Acto blade,
the orange candy cane
covering a sweet steel fletchette center,
for pseudo-seppuku kisses.
She pulls off her tee shirt,
eyes following the white, blue-veined skin
from her elbow to her wrist.

And she laughs sickly, disgusted by herself
and the extreme that is required
to snap back into reality.

When she falls into blackness,
sedentary dementia,
her answer has always been
to bleed.

IDENTITY CRISIS

Hannah Cook

Maybe I will become a librarian too.
Then we can be two librarians living
in an old house, surrounded by our books
all day. It would be better though if you
were a woman, and then we could be lesbians
disguised as spinsters. Two lesbian librarians
and nine or ten cats in a Cape Cod
at the end of a quiet small town cul-de-sac.

But I yearn for the bustle, the road noise
of the city. I would rather write the books
than shelve them, and you would make
a terrible lesbian, since I can never seem
to get your face between my legs.

Night In the Body

Gaylord Brewer

To be faithful in storm, patient of fools, tolerant of
memories and the muttering prophets,
It is needful to have night in one's body.
—Robinson Jeffers

The feet to begin,
text of their soldiering defeat,
encrypted demands.
A document of wound
on one side, wound the other.

The skin's flaming parchment.
How the sun marks,
how passes, how destroys.
How the chest burns beneath its pulse.

Then the night.
The billows of the sheet.
The summons of curtain.
The sky's cold vocabulary of fire.

The eyes closed
as if to contain, and lips,
parched and mute,
poised to inhale
language the voice will never speak.

And a faltered breath,
risen in the frame.

Me Feeling, and Him Dying

Chimena Kabasenche

Not with a formality of ballroom dancers
holding hands at the start,
but with the familiarity of ballet
where she jumps, and he moves with her.
Please hold me in balance like that,
the weight between us, but without solution—

How Skin Feels Sorrow
Wroclaw, Poland 2004
Sara Baker

The first time I thought:
something bad happened here.

The late evening walk home from my school
took some getting used to—
turning that corner in the dark,
walking quietly under the bridge,
the occasional train rattling overhead.

I would glance behind me to make sure I was alone.

The train tracks themselves required some
adjusting to as well.
How many days passed
before I could stand in front of them
and not think of people trapped in wooden cars?

One night I stepped under the bridge,
and my stomach began to itch fiercely
as if suddenly attacked by fleas.
My mind dashed straight to that dark place,
to a pregnant woman on her way to Auschwitz,
that pure hell not 200 kilometers from where I stood,
the skin of her belly stretching and burning.

Another night. More itching. And more.
I thought, surely, the very air I breathed,
the earth on which I stood was infected
by centuries of struggle and sorrow.
Yet brilliant red flowers still bloomed.
Children laughed, lovers sighed on park benches.

Amidst communist concrete
and medieval cobblestone,
it's easy to let your mind wander to the worst.
Something more practical then:
after countless wars, industry, life,
the Odra is unfit for drinking.
So the air too is tainted with the past—
a friend said unseen particles of coal inflamed my skin.
Residue of a long, thorny history, yes,
now part of mine,
lodged in the memory of my body.

BODY HEAT

Edison Jennings

On the floor, amid the clutter,
a pat of sunlight spread like butter,

sautéed the kicked-off high-heel shoes,
the boutique blouse of sequined blues,

the lingerie you had let fall—
and there you stood in nothing at all.

Time since that rich dishevelment,
found you less and less content,

until you shed constraint like heat,
dazzling but indiscreet,

that warmed, then burned and left me chilled
in the house the sun once filled,

floored with shifting pools of gold,
a grotto where I now grow old,

drifting through the gilded wrack,
grotesque of love, or love's lack.

AFTER READING ROBERT FROST'S "COME IN"

Gabby Kindell

The disco lights swirl slowly, soon they'll tire
and fluorescents will snap on with a boring hum.
Until then, a businessman lives for one more song
and the nipple of her thrusting breast

FATIGUE

Marianne Worthington

All the day long he drives
an olive green pickup, house to house,
repairing broken washers and dryers
for the Utility Company. In stifling
garages and damp basements
he fights off poodles and Chihuahuas
with sharp teeth, snotty kids,
cranky housewives whose laundry
has piled up like haystacks.

Teaching his left hand to work
after the stroke, he's an expert with tools
but the paperwork outwits him,
the pen slipping from his crippled
right fist, the dyslexia blurring
the model numbers and parts prices.

Each night he arrives home streaked
with machine grease and sweat
smelling like Winstons and gasoline,
head throbbing from exhaustion and hunger.
He chases a B.C. Powder with a shot
of Old Crow, strips to his undershorts,
straddles the tub edge to scrub with Ajax.

His mind whirrs: the mortgages, the choked
gutters, his girls on the schoolbus, his aged
mother alone in that old house, the top
floor rented out to strangers. He shakes
the blue grains from the cylinder, rubs
his nicked hands and blackened fingers
and watches the gray clumps rinse away
with the grit from another day.

❄

BARE BONES BAKER
Rebecca Brooks

BARE BONES BAKER was a landmark on Lonesome Valley Road. Wearing familiar Liberty overalls with every pocket bulging with Pepsi bottles, he walked twice a day the two miles to Sam's Grocer. About once a week, he came into our yard and asked in his faltering voice: "You gotta Pepsi, Budda?" Mom forbade us to indulge him. After all, we only got Pepsi on Saturdays.

His name was Barnard, but no one called him that. To the folks on Lonesome Valley Road, he was just Bare Bones. He never called anyone by their given name—everyone was "Budda." Bare Bones was so much a part of my childhood landscape that I never gave him much consideration beyond telling him we had no Pepsi or we didn't need our yard mowed. His sunken eyes darted back and forth when he spoke to you, and his cheeks were hollow with scattered teeth in a mouth that wrapped widely around his face. He always wore a couple of days of stubble, and a crumpled hat covered his uncombed hair. His gaunt arms and legs dangled from his body like a comic Halloween skeleton, rendering the nickname Bare Bones long before I knew him.

***

Twenty years had passed since I lived on Lonesome Valley Road. I was visiting Mom during a long vacation from my job as a reporter. Looking through Mom's old pictures one day, I found a picture of Bare Bones Baker. I hadn't known it existed. I rushed to the other room to ask Mom about the picture.

"Well," she said, "I took it one day when he asked for a Pepsi. I thought he probably never had his picture taken much. He was so tickled."

Sure enough, there was a wide, almost toothless grin on his face. But the eyes looked back at me with such a haunted look that I shuddered. As a child, I had never been *afraid* of Bare Bones, but still, after so many years, I was thoroughly disconcerted with the image of him in his overalls standing in my mom's carport. Mom said to keep the photo. She didn't understand my fascination with Bare Bones and seemed reluctant to talk about him.

Mom had always been vague when we asked her about his background, but now I sensed an opening. "Do you remember that Bare Bones was buried in his overalls? He looked so clean and crisp in the casket," I said.

Mom looked out the window to the road, and I knew she was picturing the lonely figure of a ghostly man walking up the road. "I remember," she said, but I felt she had closed the subject. Almost as an afterthought, she added, "Go talk to Johnny Jackson. He might tell you something."

"He's still around?"

"He lives on Camp Road. The old Coker house."

***

Jimmy and Johnny Jackson were the meanest boys to grow up on our road. They were a couple of years older than me, and I avoided them. I remember speaking to them only a few times—once to ask them about their curious birthdays. They were brothers and were born in the same year. Jimmy was born in early February, and Johnny was born later that year on Christmas Eve. Many people thought they were twins because they were in the same grade at school. The third grade teacher, Esther Mae Wells, quit on the spot the first day of school when she walked into her classroom and saw Jimmy in the first row on the left and Johnny in the third row.

It was my loathsome circumstance that I rode a bus to school, and, in the mornings, Jimmy and Johnny got on the bus before I did. I always tried to walk past them quickly. Sometimes they stuck their feet into the aisle to trip me, and they threw paper wads at the other kids. Besides being mean, they smelled of wood smoke and vinegar. Their clothes were few—two or three shirts and a pair of jeans each, and I never saw them wear a coat. I once overhead Mom talking on the phone once about how the boys' father had a good job but spent most of his paycheck on drinking and gambling.

Jimmy and Johnny lived down the road a bit from Bare Bones, and their favorite amusement was to heckle poor Bare Bones. It was well known that Bare Bones was afraid of snakes. About once a week, Jimmy and Johnny told the other boys on the bus of the latest trick they played on him. Their favorite was the rubber snake with a string attached on both ends. They would watch for Bare Bones to go to Sam's, then set up their prank. Jimmy would hide on one side of the road while Johnny hid on the other. Bare Bones would see the snake from several yards back and stop to throw rocks at it. He would wait until it slithered into the bushes, then continue on his way. When he got within a few feet of the boys, the snake slithered back across the road. Bare Bones would throw both hands into the air and run the other way, screaming, "Mercy me, Lord help me!" I heard Bare Bones shriek these words once when, on Halloween night, Teena Jones and I dressed as mummies and hid behind a hedge row to jump out and scare him. I was so unnerved by his reaction that I vowed never to bother the poor man again.

Jimmy and Johnny's worst trick was the Pepsi trick. Of course Bare Bones asked everyone in the neighborhood for Pepsi, but the neighbors rarely gave him one. So Jimmy and Johnny opened a new bottle of Pepsi, poured out its contents, and made up a concoction of tea, vinegar, vanilla flavoring, and whatever else they found in their mother's kitchen to give it the Pepsi color. Bare Bones was so happy at getting the Pepsi that he thanked them over and over. The boys said they could hardly keep their faces straight until Bare Bones opened the bottle and took a drink. He held the bottle up to the light and said, "I b'leve it's gone bad, yes sir, Budda, it's bad." He drank it anyway.

***

There was a tale woven among the folks on Lonesome Valley Road and at the Pleasant View School that Uncle Harve and Aunt Pearl Baker were heirs to some silver that had been buried on their property during the Civil War. Uncle Harve and Aunt Pearl were brother and sister and had raised Bare Bones. I asked Mom about it once, and she just shook her head and said, "It's not true. Nobody around here ever had any silver." But one summer Jimmy and Johnny became interested in the story, and suddenly they were all over the neighborhood, asking to do odd jobs. Mom let them bring us a load of firewood in their dad's old truck.

I watched them stack the wood in a precarious heap, and though I disliked talking to them, I had to ask, "What are y'all doin' work for?"

They looked at me with distrust. Johnny said, "We gotta earn money for Pep—."

Jimmy elbowed Johnny in the stomach. "Ain't none of your business," Jimmy said.

I had heard enough. They wanted to buy Pepsis. That meant it had something to do with Bare Bones. Two weeks later, the boys drove down the road with four cases of sixteen-ounce Pepsis in the back of their truck.

The next day, as soon as Bare Bones started on his morning walk and came into sight, the Jackson door burst open and Jimmy and Johnny ran down their driveway to meet Bare Bones. I went out onto the porch, hoping to hear what was said, but their voices were no more than distant gibberish. They walked on either side of Bare Bones, then one ran ahead and walked backwards just in front of him. It was obvious they were pleading with him for something. Bare Bones kept up his long-legged gait, and his head bobbed up and down, and then it shook from side to side. This ritual was repeated for two or three days, and I wondered what the boys wanted with him.

School started soon, and I had other boys on my mind and soon forgot about the Jackson brothers and whatever they wanted with Bare Bones.

Aunt Pearl died in late fall. There was much Bare Bones didn't understand, but he knew that Aunt Pearl was gone forever. The whole church was moved by his weeping. He sat on the front bench, bent forward with his face in his hands except when he wiped the tears with his big handkerchief. No Pepsi bottles poked out of his overalls, and his rumpled hat rested on his knee.

***

The Jackson boys had known something, but the distant connection with them had been lost by the years. Jimmy joined the army as soon as he turned eighteen and never finished high school. He was killed in a jungle in Vietnam in the last weeks of the war. Teena Jones told me once that after Johnny graduated from high school, he also joined the army. He was honorably discharged and had been married three times. Drinking was his favorite past time, she said.

Resisting the urge to call first, I drove the three miles over to Camp Road to visit Johnny. The house was an old two-story farm house. The once white house was now a weathered gray. The yard was small and neatly kept, enclosed with a board fence, also weathered gray. The porch roof was sagging but sturdy. A calico eyed me lazily from the old stone step.

"Hello," I said as I knocked.

I heard creaking floorboards from inside, then I heard latches turn, and the door slowly opened. A lean, gray-haired man with a scruffy beard and disheveled hair looked at me through familiar eyes.

"Johnny?" My voice seemed far away.

"What do you want?" His voice was friendly.

"It's me, Connie Johnson. Remember me?"

He looked at me about ten seconds before he said, "Hey there, come in, come in, where's my manners?"

He seemed genuinely glad to see me, and I followed him into the darkened living room. Heavy curtains hang at the windows and the only light came from the television. The room was neat but sparsely furnished with a worn sofa, a new-looking recliner, a pair of mahogany end tables, an old upright Wurlitzer piano, and an old safe with Helton's Department Store stenciled on the front. A black cat lounged in the middle of the sofa.

"Sit here on the couch. Do you want somethin' to drink? A Coke or some water?"

"No, thank you." By habit, my mind was searching for the one word that would describe Johnny at this moment.

"You're lookin' good. You haven't aged any. But me, I've got old," he said with sincerity.

"It's good to see you. I was sorry to hear about Jimmy."

"It's been a long time." His eyes looked through the open door onto the porch. He was far away for a moment.

"Tell me what you've been doin'," he said, turning down the TV volume.

We exchanged pleasant inquiries about each other's lives, the years making us forget that we were never friends. He told me how he had lost three wives because of his alcohol abuse but had been sober for two years. He had two children living in Georgia and proudly showed me their pictures displayed on the TV. "This here's Jimmy, and this is Mandy. I don't see 'em much, but they're good kids."

There seemed nothing more about our lives to share. I took a deep breath, "Tell me about Bare Bones."

Johnny looked a little surprised, but a smile came to his face. "Ol' Bare Bones Baker. The strangest man I ever knowed."

"Tell me about the silver that Harve and Pearl were suppose to have."

Johnny looked at me a few moments, the old traces of suspicion in his eyes. Then he smiled and said, "There weren't no silver. All they had was an old silver plated box. Harve took Pearl to the store one day, and we dug holes all in that yard, but all we found was that box."

"That's all? Just an old silver box?"

"That was it 'cept for the piece of paper in the box."

"What piece of paper?"

"It had writin' on it and was kind of faded, but I kept it. It's right here in the safe."

Johnny opened the safe and took out an envelope. It held a folded piece of paper and Bare Bones' obituary. I slowly unfolded the paper. The writing seemed old-fashioned and was completely faded in places. I tried to read it, but could only make out the words "alcohol," "needles," and "bed."

"What does it mean?"

He studied my face for a moment. "It's instructions for an abortion." Johnny hesitated. "With knittin' needles. But this one failed."

I looked at him with uneasiness, trying to put together in my mind all the old pieces to the puzzle. "Pearl?"

"Yeah, she was his mother."

"His father?"

"Well, I don't really know. But some say it was Harve."

I slumped down on the couch, staring at Johnny and then back at the paper. *My mom knew. She knew all along.*

"I'll take that Coke now."

We talked some more, and as I was going out the door, I thought of the word for Johnny: *He's gentle. He's a gentle man.* Somewhere through the remnants of lost years, the harshness and the bitterness had given away to something else. Impulsively, I gave him a hug. Wood smoke and vinegar drifted into my head, but I didn't know if it was real or a memory. He was holding the black cat, and we laughed as it jumped down.

***

The hill was steep, and I had to slow down. The tombstones stood out starkly against the blue sky. It wasn't a very big cemetery, and I soon found Bare Bones' grave close to Harve's and Pearl's. There were no flowers at his resting place, but there was a nice stone recording the simple life of Barnard James Baker. I set a Pepsi bottle holding a single red rose on the granite base. I knelt down and traced the lettering with my fingers. "This is for you, Barnard," I whispered.

The wind picked up a bit, and I thought I heard a faltering but distinct voice, "Gotta Pepsi, Budda?"

DEVELOPMENT
Leslye Stewart Ford

Under the porch before the storm drove pellets of rain
through the wooden boards, I showed Dusty Thornton my
pink seven-year-old nipples. After, we ran to his basement
and rummaged through his father's army rucksack for sugar
rations, longing for the sticky wetness on our tongues, the
way it disappears.

*

My mother's breasts were dried
of milk with the help of a needle.
I never touched them, but saw her
in the bathtub, the pinky-brown
areolas against her porcelain skin.

*

I keep waiting for the change to happen:
my breasts, larger than my mother's were
at my age, swelling as hers are now.
When you're pregnant, she says,
they'll change, expand, along
with feet and ankles. But I've
seen this happen with Emily: C's
balloon to D's, and then, after
the babies have sucked at the nipple,
the breasts are smaller than before
And God knows they don't bounce.

*

Ten: I long for curves.
Thirteen: Shame. Girls budding in the locker room. Shame

for their bodies. Shame for my
pre-pubescent body.
Fifteen: He discovers me in the front seat of his car. I dis-
cover me under his tongue.
Seventeen: There is no fat on my body. Size: 0. Breasts:
barely an A. Bikinis. Elation.
I dream of Kate Moss.
Nineteen: Changes. Thighs swell. Dimples come at twenty.
Twenty-one: Hiding. I don't own a swimsuit. No lingerie.
Make love with the lights out.
Twenty-five: I will not be my mother. I will not be Kate or
Wynona or Sarah Jessica. But
I cannot walk past the mirror without sneering.

Face at Forty

Linda R. Bell

Hidden from dawn
she opens her arms
to the world
and leans to the light,
reaching once more
for the undreamed of truth,
never expecting an
overnight conversion.

The soft, filtered morning
mirrors her reflection:
for the first time in months
she sees cheekbones.

Above neckrings of smiles
she wears wrinkles of wisdom,
creases earned
from miles of crisscrossing
the fragile bridge of herself.

Below fine grey strands
of experience
lie indentations—
underscores of knowledge,
the essence of one vital vision,
the landscape of her dreams—

and philosophical eyes,
the color of wild lupine.

There is no silence
to her life,
only cherished survival:
A certain eloquence
fortressed by tranquility and zeal,
imprinted with vibrant,
untarnished optimism.

She is never a prisoner
of time,
and only rarely
of perceptions.

As the pages of light unfold
she gains a fingerhold
on the border of the day
and we see
by the outline of her life
that age comes to us all
one hour
at
a
time.

ELEMENTAL SESTINA

Heather Joyner Spica

It must have snowed the day you were born...
I arrived in lesser weather, street vents steaming.
Sustained by your mother's blood, you emerged
into the bluster and rust of Detroit, iron-willed.
I flowed into being like gin, like jazz
let loose in nearby Greenwich Village.

And like jazz, I'm all over the place,
snow-blown notes adrift in sound.
Draining the gin dry, I leave crescents
of steam, my breath against glass.
You tell me we'll rust in this dampness...
I am certain our blood will keep us warm.

Blood the red of violent poppies,
a jazz beat in your glance, the tracery of veins.
Your rust-colored eyes take me in,
and I dare not snow on this parade
knowing steam, the rhythm between us
is as potent as gin... if not more so.

I think of your gin-smooth skin,
blood driven as if pulsing with steam
not by that muscle we connect with love
or by the jazz that makes us tick and blink

and brave relentless snow to again scrape rust
from what's been hidden.

Now that I look at you, I imagine rust
flourishing like vines, gin-ripe berries
up from snow in Spring, drawing moisture:
blood from the buzzing soil.
Now the jazz... music I thought I'd forgotten
has been sung in the steam of your voice.

Rising like steam, minutes dissipate
into rust... the present and what it becomes
a kind of raw, improvisational jazz.
I toast you with gin and my liquid gaze,
our blood pitching in time
with snow-blind desire.

Here, your steam heat heart, my gin-shot soul:
both a rust-dark shade of blood
as strains of jazz come together in falling snow.

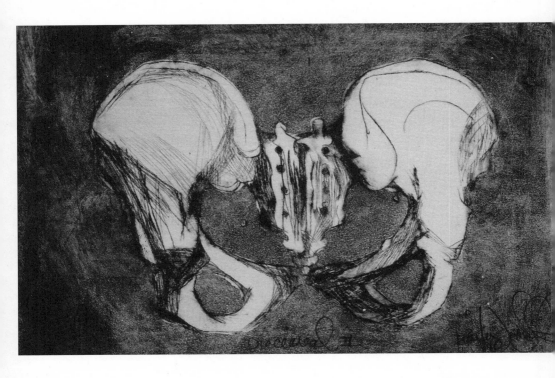

UNTITLED
Karley J. Sullivan

Invader

Susan A. Wright

The afternoon I learned I was going deaf
I sat at the stoplight, feeling the vibrations
Of the red Honda's bass from five cars away.
If they don't want their hearing, I'll take it.

At home before the mirror, staring at my ear,
I knew others would see a young woman in jeans—
An old young one with a tiny wedge of plastic
Soon to buzz in her ear like an inverse head phone.

Resentment burns my chest at the sight of Ipods
Or at the soundwaves crashing over my house
From passing cars and backyard parties.
If they don't want their hearing, I'll take it.

From the age of ten, I horded my hearing,
Eschewing walkmans, sticking fingers in my ears,
Only to have my body betray me, unleashing a genetic invader
To pillage and rape the gateway into my soul.

❊

The Failing Light

Jay N. Helmstutler

It will rise. Then fall. And fall. And keep falling.
It will rise and then fall and will not rise again.

He knows it, as he watches the flame of the candle, rising, falling, but then rising back up, as the flame of any candle should. He knows his broken part will not work like the flame; it may rise, quickly fall, but once fallen, will not rise again.

Looking at himself from the outside, he sees a figure sitting alone on the edge of a bed, watching a candle as it burns across the room. The only light in the room other than the flame of the candle is the light coming from the hallway. It seeps in through the crack in the doorway along with the noises from the kitchen. There is the sound of the refrigerator opening and closing, followed by the clanging of glassware. He listens for a pouring sound, as of drinks being poured, but instead hears the sound of her voice humming a song. It is a song he recognizes from the car ride over, the last song on the radio before they had arrived at her home. A love song, it had filled him with the same sense of dread as the love scene in the movie they had gone to. Now that they were back from their evening together, there was no escaping the dreaded scenario. She had already lit the candle and left the room to make the drinks, after showing him the pictures from her life.

If only she hadn't shown him those pictures.

His eyes sink down from the candle atop the bookcase to the place amongst the books where he had seen her filing back the photo album. He wills his mind across the room toward the album, returning in his mind to the section she had turned hurriedly through. Here, in the section with the half-torn pictures, all that remains of the person cut out is a hand or perhaps just a shadow. Now, each one of those shadows begins to multiply, spreading its multitudes out along the walls. The shadows take the forms of bodies, the body of the figure cut out from the doctored photographs, melded with bodies from other doctored photographs perhaps in some other album she had yet to show him. And as the shadows begin to move, their movements become the shadows of her lovers' past performances—performances he finds himself up against tonight. He knows that he will lose. To lose is his fate amongst the shadows. In the rooms of lovers past, they have conspired against him time and again, turning situations ripe with promise and pleasure into scenarios of horror and lost hope. Always there have been shadows playing along the walls, because always his partners have had partners prior to him, and hence a standard of comparison has always been in place. He could never measure up. He could never even *get* it up without his partner's tedious help; and if he did get help, he would only soon thereafter go limp. That was his history in rooms like this: a history filled with shadows plaguing the walls, with ever-present shadows of doubt plaguing his mind, and with partners who would themselves become living shadows by night's end, having already begun to shy away from him on discovering that he didn't, in fact, function like other men.

Such had been the case with his last partner, whose harsh words somehow find echo amongst present walls, cast out from one shadow for the other across the room to catch: *You have a problem. You definitely have a problem.* The memory of his last humiliation, wielded like a plaything to re-humiliate him here: that first and final night with a partner particularly cruel. *You should be standing at attention,* she had barked, the frustrated words now mocked by the beastly shapes hovering above him, who have mobilized into visual taunt: the figure of a man projected onto the ceiling, its one hand cocked to forehead in military salute, its other wrapped around a ramrod member.

And this is only the beginning, he thinks. *The beginning of the torments. First from the shadows, then eventually from her. For surely, she will show me no mercy. If only. If only she needed to show me no mercy, were there some miraculous chance not to fail. Always, that one little chance not to fail, to work just like any other man.* He looks down amongst the shadows that are bearing down on him, toward the broken machine in his pants, praying that it will not fail him this time. Praying that for once it will work like the hero's in the love scene, as an afterthought, a reflex, an instinct not lost through over-contemplation of every move he should be making, were he physically able to make every move he had in mind. He has given up hoping the problem is all in his mind. He knows it is real, and that he has somehow been destined to fail in these matters. It is only a matter of time before she finds out. Before it becomes her cross to bear for the night, and for however many other nights she will lie with him before finally realizing, admitting, that there is something terribly wrong with his body, and then rejecting it, along with him, since there is no separating the two. Or rather, because the two are completely separated—from his body, that cannot be turned on, to his mind, that he cannot turn off.

His thoughts are interrupted by her footsteps moving toward the room. His heart starts beating faster, but he tries his best to compose himself as she gently nudges the door open with her foot and carefully enters the room with two glasses of wine balanced in her hands. He looks up at her face as the light from the hallway scatters the shadows that have been taunting him while she was away. "Did I leave you alone too long?" she asks, handing him one of the glasses.

"Not at all," he says. "I was just entertaining myself watching this candle."

"You like it?" she asks with pride and pleasure in her voice. "To me, it's like a piece of art." With new eyes, he looks at the candle, a wax sculpture of a man and a woman locked in an embrace. The two figures hold each other so tightly that their parts blend together, bleeding into one another as the ember burns from the tops of their heads.

"Would you mind if I play some music for us?" the woman asks.

"Sure," he answers.

"Do you have any preferences?"

"Not really. I'll leave it up to you."

He watches her as she walks over to the stereo that sits in the middle part of the bookcase. The shadows use the opportunity to reconfigure themselves along the walls. After a moment, the notes of a slow song begin to fill the room, scattering the shadows as she turns around and returns to where he sits. They sit next to each other on the bed, watching the candle burn as the music saturates the midnight air.

I should have been looking forward to this, he thinks, *but I've only been afraid. If only I didn't have to be afraid.* The woman sighs, shifting her glass from one hand to the other. Her gesture disrupts his thoughts. She leans her head against his shoulder, her gaze fixed on the burning candle. He leans his head upon hers. *One last moment of tranquility,* he thinks. *Let me take this one last moment and hold it.* But as the flame dies down and reminds him of his weakness, he is sure that he will fall very soon.

How should I tell her? he thinks. *How can I explain to her the complexity of my problem? How deep it runs, how I can't really help it, how it's been my curse for so long. How I've been told by doctors that it's all in my head, but how they've failed me in not believing me, because I know that it's real. I know my body better than anyone, and I know I'm not making it up. I know I'm destined not to make love to the one I love, that it is just the way I am made and meant to be. Any futures with the ones before, un-made before they had even begun; and yet, I could see no future in any of them. She is different; perhaps the Future Herself. If only that future did not have to end tonight.*

"What are you thinking about?" she asks, interrupting his train of thought. He lifts his head up from hers, as if awakened from a trance. He avoids eye contact with her, as he shakes his head and answers, "Nothing. Nothing." He feels as if she has learned his thoughts, as if she knows of the helplessness inside him. As if she can sense the shadows closing him in, and the fact that he has nowhere to escape. She takes his chin in her hand, slowly turning his head toward hers, as she looks directly into his eyes. "Tell me what's on your mind." He looks into her eyes, looking as helpless as he feels, knowing there is no escape from what he must tell her. Knowing he must try to put it into words, even if he has never been able to with anyone before.

"Look, there are things that you may not want to know right now. Actually, it will be better for us if you don't know about them."

"What do you mean, there are things?" she asks patiently.

"I mean, there are things that I can't really tell you. I'm afraid it's going to hurt what we have." He pauses, looking back at the candle. Then he continues. "What we have is so valuable. It's so meaningful to me. I really want it to go somewhere. I don't want to lose it that easily."

"What do you mean, lose it that easily?"

"I mean, look, I can't tell you what's going on with me. There are things about me it's better not to know. But I'm afraid you'll find out sooner or later, so I want to tell you. I'm just afraid you'll let me go once you find out about it. I'm afraid I'm going to make you disappointed."

He looks into her eyes, awaiting an answer. She looks puzzled, as if she has questions, but stays quiet. She turns her head toward the candle and continues watching it quietly. Then she puts her head back onto his shoulder, and slowly whispers, "You need to calm down."

"No, I think I really need to tell you. I can't calm down. I am worried. I'm anxious. I can't calm down, do you understand? I need to tell you this."

She lifts her head up from his, takes the remote from its place beside the bed, and uses it to stop the music. "If you really feel like telling me, then go ahead and say it. I'll listen to you," she says. She turns her head toward him and shows that she is ready to listen.

He looks down. "Look, I really need to let you know, straightforward, before anything happens between us," he says. "I have some problems, you know? No matter how much I want you, I can't physically satisfy you. Do you understand? I have trouble staying..." The flame of the candle falters, making a hissing sound. He starts his words over again. "I've been called 'malfunctional.'" He sighs deeply and continues. "I've always feared, and have been told, that my parts don't work quite right." He looks down in shame and waits for the laughter of the shadows, certain that it will pierce the heavy silence at any moment. His thoughts are loud inside his head. *I don't know where it can go from here*, he thinks. *What is she thinking? Is she thinking like me that it's over, our future, before it has even begun? Is she thinking how she can get out of this situation and not have to see me again? Please let her say something. The silence is too heavy to bear.* He breaks the momentary silence with his own impatient voice. "What do you think of all this?" he says. "I understand if you want to say goodbye. It's not your fault. I won't take it personally. You have every right to stop this here, at this point in time."

He lifts his head up, mustering the courage to look into her eyes. He is surprised to see the peaceful look on her face. The smile there. She reaches out her hand to touch his and begins to caress his fingers. She brings his hand next to her lips and kisses it softly. She holds his hand next to her heart and whispers, "All that matters to me is to be with you. All that matters is you."

As she holds his hand next to her heart, she looks at the candle. "You think a lot, don't you?" she says. "You've got to find a way to calm down."

And how is it, he wonders. How is it that in this room with the shadows and the memory of lovers past, she could take the time to hold my hand instead of rushing forward or rejecting me for my dysfunctions; how is it that in my humiliation and fear she can calm me and give peace to my senses and tell me that everything is fine? How is it? How is it that she is my future, that she would want a future with this lopsided creature, with this man still a boy of body, still a child of fear with this mind so preoccupied with shortcomings, imperfections, things I cannot overcome? How is it? How is it, and how will it be if I ever make it inside of her, how will it be if it is over before it starts like every time I have done this before? How will it be that she will still be with me then?

The voice inside his head, the voice of doubt, forces an apology from his mouth. "I'm sorry," he says. "You don't deserve this."

"There's nothing to be sorry for."

"I wish. I just wish I could be normal. Because if I was I would... "

"Take it out of your head. Just be here with me. Here, come lay beside me."

"I'm sorry."

"There's nothing to be sorry for. Just lay here in my arms." He puts his head on her chest, feeling her breathing beneath him, in and out. "Just calm down. Listen," she says. He closes his eyes, feeling the skin of her neck with his fingers, hearing her heartbeat between her breaths, between her breasts. She brings her hand up and strokes the back of his head with her hand, a stroke of surrender, coaxing out the shadows, and all thoughts of time and space. Coaxing him back into his body, into himself, from the place he has been watching from afar for so long, hiding; tonight; yesternight; forever till this moment, a stranger, until finally made familiar, till an observer made participant, a third person finally made first, whose very first words address her in second person. "I can feel your heart beat," I say. And in your tenderness, your patience, I am more than a living malady, more than the sum of my individual parts, more than I have ever been and capable of, more than I have ever been capable of before. All of my befores are nothing compared to my now, my now that is my now and my future at the same time, and my past that means nothing and that I cannot even remember in the instant you begin to lay me in your arms. And I believe. I believe and leave my body behind, not one part at a time, but all at once, so that all of the parts come together and are discarded at once. I can throw it all away because I don't need it anymore, knowing that your love and patience are limitless, knowing you will take me as I am, as the sum of body parts I have become and have now discarded. So that now I am just naked me, naked inside and out but with inside and out being all the same, with being inside of you the same as being outside, with being a part of you being the same as being apart from you, because my body is in the flame of the candle, scorching its imperfections away, even as I can feel you beside me and your hands over my skin. You feel inside of me as I lay on top of you, turning the tides, forgetting the currents of fear and just living and being alive as I should and have every right to, using my body as it was made to be used, against the body of the one I know I love. And yes. I love you. I already know and the shadows know, too, and that is why they have scurried away, the only shadow now being ours cast against the wall as we let the candle define us, and we embody it and surrender our bodies to the process of melting away and not thinking, because the tops of our heads are gone, and our brains are gone, and there will only be our bodies once our head has burned itself away. And once there is only our bodies, there will only be the motion that bodies are supposed to make, as we are making now, as, as, can you believe, as we are already making now. And I suddenly realize I am no longer watching from afar, no longer an observer of myself and my lover, but my lover and myself, two people at once, two bodies as one, the bodies of the candle, I am, I am, we are, we have done it. We have overcome. Overcome. And as we sit two bodies on our couch in a future time and place, staring at the half-burnt candle in our mantle, our relic from that night, our life together both behind and in front of us, an image plays below our gaze on the television: two lovers in perfect harmony, in the midst of their love scene, the woman on top of the not-faltering man. The television is not on. Only soft music in the background, two glasses of wine on the table before us, our reflection in the television as we watch ourselves making love.

At the Seams

Liz McGeachy

At first it was only a loose finger, wobbling
distractedly on the lump of her hand until it

plopped to the carpet at the leg of her chair.
She snatched it up and stuck it into her purse

before anyone could see, vowing to sew it on that
very evening. But then it was the ear, suddenly

splashing into her soup at the restaurant where he stood
her up, then a couple of toes she never even realized

she had left rolling down the echoing hallway.
Soon it became impossible to ignore the ragged

split at her hip joint and how cumbersome it was to
maneuver the noodling appendages hanging on by the

merest of threads. She attempted patchwork, wanting to believe
the stitches unnoticeable, but the unraveling persisted.

She knew she would eventually be found immovable,
undone—a scattering of unhinged body parts like

stones spilt on a cold bed.

LILIES

Elizabeth Howard

Blood gushed from my nose onto
the garden lilies, the clods,
my feet speckled like guinea
eggs hidden in the grape-arbor
nest, onto the linoleum as I
ran screeching for mother,
who left potatoes frying,
the baby crawling about.
Cold wet cloth to nose,
forehead, back of neck,
and the flow was soon checked.
I lay on the baby's pallet,
blanket satin against my face,
practiced breathing,
unbreathing.

A school boy leaned over the porch
railing, nose dripping, a red
puddle in the dirt, teacher
frantic to locate parents.
Three days later, we gave
coins to buy lilies, saw
him in a satin-lined box.

Awakened at night, blood pouring
onto the pillow, I screamed.
Mother came with wet cloths,

placed icy scissors on my nape,
raised my arms above my head,
all the remedies she'd heard of
until the flow was stanched.
Hours after she left,
I lay alone in the dark,
warm red rain falling softly
on small dry clods,
guttering, puddling.
Behind my eyelids,
the image of a face
framed in white satin,
a lily in the cupped hands.

How Female Often Works

Carole Urmy

body,
assembly line,
endless ride.

wound up
let go
she cracks,
broken cargo.

repaired,
recycled,
rescrewed,
endless journey.

she roosts,
tired cage of flesh,
producing eggs.

FATHER TREY MAKES
AN OFFER

Marilyn Kallet

At the friary lunch Father Trey asks,
"Do you have laundry?"
Lean, young Kevin Costner.
We three women poets nod,
"Yes!"
"I'd be happy to do your wash," he says.
"Leave it on the porch."

"No thank you," I gulp.
When he leaves we gasp,
"Oh my God!"
Margie whispers red panties.
Jill has been lounging in pink
polka-dotted birthday jammies.
No, no, no, Father Trey.
You will not be handling my
black Barely There bra.

You will not fold my blue
silk bikini bottoms.
You stride like Bull Durham,
Father, and looks
rarely deceive.
What penance makes you seek
soiled underthings?

If you insist,
we could go down
to the nunnery basement
with its old vibrating
wash and spin,
gas-fired pilot lights,
huge hot dryers,
lie on the sturdy table for folding
holy briefs
on top of immaculate towels
bathe each other with caresses
beneath the hanging jello mold
of our Mother of Consolation.

We'd weep mutual tears of absolution
beneath the "Cup of Joy" blessing card,
and—you know what's coming—
cleanse each other deeply
with Judeo-Christian tongues.

YOUNG GIRLS AS PACKAGES
Richard Remine

In the End, Will There Be Light?

Charlotte Pence

Some wonder, "Who created this world?"
But I wonder who will destroy it.
Who will skin the last needle
from the Carolina pine, steal
the Buick's battery from the drive?
And after my body folds into this earth,
who will allow my black gloves,
thin without the agency of busy hands,
to remain flat on the hall table?
Now, my keys lie on them, force them
to this earth with its weddings and wars
and the immutable transiency of both.
Surely these gloves won't destroy the world,
but maybe the child who sewed them;
or the frustrated man who loaded them;
or me, thinking two bucks was too much to pay.
I'm waiting for them to walk away
one day like a good pair of socks
as I wait to walk away one last time.
In my dreams, everything dreams, even
these gloves, and so, I bend toward the grass
when one jumps from my pocket,
take a moment to notice how today,
as most days, the world concerns itself

with living. Even the ants are complicit
on this sunny, winter morning,
immolating all their might and strength
to what they know of tomorrow,
to the lightning-white sacks of eggs
held high above their darkened heads.

HEAD WOUNDS
Jack Rentfro

HIS MOTHER HAD been sound asleep for many hours by this time. Her generation knew full well that nothing good ever came from being up at such an hour. But he could never sleep, and this night home from college found him rummaging through what he called "the National Trust." From a Beatles' lyric—just a walk-in closet. But, as a child, he had found refuge there, sitting on a stool, reading an old set of Compton's Encyclopedias, and breathing the musty air of knick-knacks and heirlooms stacked along the shelves.

Daddy's .32 automatic pistol was exactly where he remembered—in a Hav-a-Tampa cigar box jammed atop the obsolete reference books. Other males in the family had made off long ago with the heavier firearms that Daddy, the last horsetrader of the 20th century, had acquired buying and selling toward the success that killed him. The .32 was a delicate little piece of murderously precise engineering, its ivory grip browned from past owners' palms. The clip still carried a full load of brass cartridges the old man surely had thumbed into the magazine himself. The boy pulled back the bolt and was satisfied by the *snick* as the top round in the clip slid home.

He took the pistol outside and sat on the rear stoop. Between his feet was the inscription "B GANT" he had fingertipped in the wet cement the year Daddy added a backyard sidewalk. He had just read *Look Homeward, Angel*, Thomas Wolfe's exuberant paean to brotherhood and youth. The protagonist of that story, Eugene Gant, grieved for his older, wiser brother, Ben, who died before telling Eugene how to make sense of the world.

The air was thick and sweet from the wisteria clumped around the backyard. Frogs added a minstrel show chorus to the hot, black night. He toggled off the safety. The barrel of the little automatic was cool against cheek. He pressed the bore into his temple, then into a squinting eye-socket as if seeking an itch to scratch.

The big Army Model 1911 Colt .45 would have been the way to go—no missing with that baby—no chance of being rendered a drooling slackwit for that poor widow in the back bedroom to take care of in her waning years. It was the one Daddy had used to baptize him early in the shock and power of firearms. He remembered one of their early gun training sessions. The boy's fingers could barely reach around the grip when Daddy showed him the proper way to hand someone a pistol. It nearly jumped out of the boy's hands when they went shooting that time on Chilhowee Mountain. He had emptied a carton of blunt, blue slugs into an old piling out in the mountaintop lake, splintering it to a nub. He aimed the .45 at the clouds and pictured the wads of lead lofting into the atmosphere. Before pulling the trigger, he asked his father something that was bothering him: whether or not shooting at clouds might kill an angel. Daddy got that faraway pondering look. "Well," he snickered, "you might wing one."

A president, a brother and a father, all gone, and here he was home for a weekend from college, sitting in the dark on the back stoop of the family home on a sickeningly humid night pulsing with katydids and frogs. With only a .32—never mind that was good enough for James Bond.

Feeling the implacability of it—his own doom in his hand. It was like holding his shadow, like tricking the Devil into a snipe-hunting sack. Jerking the gun away from his temple, he pointed the gun straight up and emptied it as fast as he could squeeze the trigger. The muzzle flash strobe-lit the back yard, and then all went dark again. No wounded night angels fell flopping to the ground like slaughtered chickens. He thrilled in the resulting cacophony of neighborhood dogs and porch lights flicking on around the block, then worried the clamor would rouse his mother.

Stepping back inside, he heard his mother's bedroom door click shut. Cocooned away in her room in the air-conditioning *hummm*, she had already dismissed the disturbance: It must have been that late night TV her boy stayed up watching when he couldn't sleep. He helped himself to a long pull of Daddy's Old Crow from the liquor cabinet, gagging to hold it down, and went to bed in his old room. He peeked through the curtain as a vehicle crept by in front of the house, a constable car with its coon light sweeping yards on both sides of the street.

Covers pulled up to his nose, he lay awake, dreading the moan of a train whistle sure to come about now. There was always a wee hours train rumbling through town. Without the comforting white noise of his college apartment fan by the bed, he slept badly, jostled from one phantasmic dream to another by sirens and car horns. The bed he writhed in had been his brother's before he went away to college. That was when the boy inherited it. And it was this same bed from which he was awakened with the news that his brother was dead. Killed when a train hit the car he was in near his Army base in Alexandria, Virginia. Impossibly, so it seemed, exactly five years to the day after President Kennedy was murdered. When the whistle sounded at last, he listened hard, imagining it was the very train that had brought his brother home on his last leave. The same mystery train that would take his life and then carry home the body a few days after that.

Bedroom ceiling decorations spun into his delirium: a luminescent full moon face; quarter moon profile with face; a Telstar satellite with antennae; a grinning planet wearing a Tom Terrific funnel hat; a ringed, laughing Saturn. Mama had pasted these glow-in-the-dark novelty items over the bed for his brother when he was a child. A celebration of America's next frontier conquest. Now, they were the mocking iconography for a cold galaxy into which he wished to tumble headlong, alone, on an infinite orbit of the cosmos.

Before rummaging around in the National Trust, he had smoked some of the pot in his brother's things the Army returned to the family. There was only a hit or two left from the nickel baggie tucked behind a ball of thin black socks inside the shiny black brogans in the hardshell suitcase that contained what the Army called his "personal effects." Which included the boy's birthday cards to his brother. The boy had hoarded his brother's reciprocal cards in the desk next to the bed. One, subtexting the brother's comedy routine that the family was actually Jewish, was cruelly postscripted: "Watch out for Eichmann. He's back in town." There was another he had sketched out with a ballpoint pen on a piece of Army memo paper: a cartoon of himself during boot camp at Fort Campbell—he the skinny, insignificant, shaven-pated buck private, mop in hand, standing shyly in the first sergeant's office. A talk balloon above the wispy little figure reads: "Please, sergeant, sah! Ah gots 15 cents and it's Satiddy night! Kin ah go to town and get me a Coke?" From behind his desk, the burly, bulldog-faced, brushcut noncom the size of a mountain range shoots back: "Shut yer goddam mouth and finish cleaning those latrines!" The Thanksgiving card had this trademark, cartoon cipher soldier sweeping up the hallway of the international officers' billet. A swarthy, mustached officer dashes by, buttoning his "NATO" stenciled dress jacket. The little figure in fatigues is saying, "Excuse me, sir! Where are you from and where are you going?" "Turkey and dressing!" explains the exchange officer's talk balloon.

The boy wanted to know how he would get his own head injury, that most perfect token of the indiscriminate force's driving existence. A scalp scar being the only recognition point for the chemical-stinking chunk of government cheese they sent home in a dull gray aluminum transfer case. The boy desired senselessness, a step into oblivion where there was neither remembering nor the pain that it brought. A return to an insensate *aleph* point that preceded and presupposed everything. Before the cataclysmic disconnect that had happened to the country only to swing by five years later like a comet that hit only his family. Because both were hopelessly lost and new maps needed to be drawn.

On his brother's last leave, the boy was worshipful as a 15-year-old could be to his 23-year-old brother. He was riveted to the scant decorations on the enlisted man's Class A uniform breast pocket. Next to the marksman's Maltese cross was a bright yellow 'I'm a Junior Railroader for Southern!' pin, likely just cadged off the conductor. With this gentle spoof of military glory, he had put his personal imprint on such a prosaic concept as duty. Subversive humor, as with the holiday cards, seemed to show the way to happily endure the temporary ordeal of national service. Which was all the more absurd by 1968, when the enemy's surprise Tet Offensive had deflated any last pretense the war was just or winnable. But this was a soldier who also could teach him not only about Thomas Wolfe, William Faulkner, D.H. Lawrence, Flannery O'Connor, Leo Tolstoy

and Fyodor Dostoevsky but the Beatles, Ray Charles, Bob Dylan, Stan Free-
burg, Ernie Kovacs, the Smothers Brothers, Steve Allen and Woody Allen
as well. His worldview even had a place for cracker stand-up Brother Dave
Gardner. Gardner's bit about selling water to Yankees was "a riot." "You're
a riot!" the older brother would yell at the boy when he said something
funny. Then, with a burlesque slap to the forehead, he would let loose a
hearty "Hoo-Hah!"—just like a Don Martin *Mad Magazine* cartoon character.

Few had the nerve for the private viewing offered at the funeral
home. Back at the house later, the old girlfriend from college careened
into the rear bedroom where the family took respite from the larger gath-
ering in the kitchen. "It's not him!" she shrieked, sick with it, making
sounds that chilled the boy's soul.

Various fantasies took flight among the bereaved, except Daddy, who
would have none of it and just sat in the corner, sipping bourbon. These
fictions were comforting in those raw hours. Like the one that made the
death a grotesque clerical error stemming from identification problems,
meaning the body at the funeral home was actually someone else's loved
one. Or the theory that the evil government had kidnapped him for use in
some imperialist plot, which through his irrepressible combination of wit
and personality, would be exposed. The preferred story among the wiseass
beatniks who also had congregated at the house was that his brother had
just had enough of all the bullshit and was on the lam in Marrakech,
smoking hashish with Beat poet Paul Bowles. And on it went.

Some years later, the driver in the accident—his brother's off-base
roommate—would be brave enough to meet the family and explain they
simply didn't see the train. It was one of those unmarked, country cross-
ings and it was foggy, just past midnight, and they had been drinking
after going to a movie near their base in Alexandria, Virginia.

The army's mortuarial people, being somewhere on a par with back-
woods taxidermists, had patched him together by a kind of dead reck-
oning. The Army strongly advised against an open casket. An officer explained that, unfortunately, the only photo the morticians had to work
with was the black-and-white boot camp ID in which all the burrheaded
GIs look like terrified beagle puppies.

The girlfriend couldn't find the asterisk-shaped scalp scar from a childhood stunt in which he fell off a chest of drawers onto his head. It seemed to have been scrambled amid the larger insult caused by 120,000 tons of Southern Railroad. And the bandaging and cavity putty. "What about his chipped tooth?" the boy asked, remembering the pool ball he lobbed at his brother for no good reason, nuancing forever his brother's smirk. There was no answer; just another round of wailing that came in pained bursts all night from the bedroom where his mother would be sleeping alone in just a few more years.

Anniversaries of that day in November came; decades passed after that night on the back stoop. The boy sought subtler ways to blow his head off.

There were always mass media retrospectives about the national apocalypse and the boy eventually subsumed his grief into the nation's, which, over the years, became quite an industry. In its never-ending scavenger hunt to dilate and expose every conceivable aspect of the country's trauma, television at last brought the nation what it slavered for—the JFK autopsy photographs. Through diagrams and blow-ups and analyses of ballistics and neurosurgery, the gaping head wound was thrust into the collective living room. Talking heads pointedly noted that a section of the brain was inexplicably absent, apparently due to clandestine surgery rather than the explosive effect of a slug from a $12.78 mail order rifle. Amateur commentators suggested something mystically was afoul with the absconsion of the president's brain. Or that Kennedy, like the boy's brother, might be alive, kidnapped by the CIA and held in a secret complex a mile below the fields of Gettysburg. The once heroic profile, now deflated like an old volleyball, reminded the boy of a tabloid newspaper's claim that Castro had Kennedy's head and kept it alive through voodoo, tormenting his old nemesis every morning with smoke rings from his ever-present cigar. A perverse satire floated by a late '60s underground publication had suggested the ascendant vice president utilized the still-warm cranial cavity for sexual release.

It started with reports from Dallas of one unpardonable crime and paraded on five more years to the morning when Daddy woke him to say why he would not be going to school that morning. And then wouldn't leave the boy's mind for the rest of his life.

Cross-contaminated memories, juxtaposed forever: a Dallas motorcade and a nameless train crossing outside Alexandria, Virginia. A mythically imbued leader who committed U.S. troops to a little brushfire war against the communists in Indochina and a young footsoldier idolized by his little brother who had figured, as long as he was already in the military, why not escalate the voluntary adventure to its supremely absurd culmination. Only to be nearly decapitated, a mere transportation industry statistic, before he got to Vietnam.

Reversed boots; marijuana in the black brogans. An eternal flame at Arlington, Virginia, and a plain brass plaque on a hillside in Tennessee glimmering like an eternal Jack O'Lantern. Shining and void.

More presidents would lose their minds. The boy continued to fill the hole in his head with whatever he could find, even emptiness, when that would do.

OCTOBER TENTH: FOR MY FIRST SON

Libby Falk Jones

At a surprise T'ai Chi class (the yoga
    teacher was sick) I breathe in, hold,
        breathe out, willing my ribs to

expand, focusing on the knot in the
    floorboard, circling my hands over
        the energy flame in my navel

as eighteen years ago today
    I panted your life into life,
        my fingers circling my knotted

belly, my focus down and
    out, my core expanding, my
        center sliding forward, until

there you sat, upright
    in the doctor's palm, your arms
        circling the universe.

SEXTANT

Curt Rode

When I look straight ahead
All I see of myself
Are my glasses and a hint
Of the nose they sit on,
And a hand now and then
As I type or drive
Or adjust my ubiquitous frames.

Yet somehow,
When my head is up,
I'm expected to love myself,
That someone I can't—
Without contorting for mirrors
Or sitting for photographs—
Ever completely see.
What a leap of faith.

Is it any wonder
We unfold ourselves
Across each other's beds?
So these are the Tropics
Of Shoulder and Calf.
And these the trails
To the fragrant valleys.
To chart our blind navigations.
To map the fogged rivers back.

In the Dark

Margrethe Krogh

I always knew my body would betray me
The way I drank it senseless
Smoked it full of toxins

The way I slept with that man
And that one

Pushing it to limits I wanted to transcend

Always wanting more
To feel more
See more
Taste more and more and more

And now in the quiet days of that past's distant future
It tells me this time
It's not me in control

The tests come back
Positive
Final
Six months, maybe a year

And I talk to my body at night
Whispering in the dark house

In the Dark

I don't blame you
Just try to understand
I couldn't get enough
Everything was just too delicious

My body doesn't answer
It just breathes, remembers
And dreams in the dark.

MISSING

Felicia Mitchell

My mother is missing a breast.
At Sunday dinner, no concentrated sugar allowed,
she pulls the fabric of her blouse and lets it fall
against her deflated chest.
                                        And then she points
to the other breast that is not missing,
the one not even I, her daughter, suckled,
the one poised there like a teardrop.
I tell her *they* had to cut it off, that missing breast,
and smile and point to her plate.
"Here," I say. "You'll want to eat your turkey."
But she won't eat this white meat
pulled clean from the bone, soft and tender,
only yellow pudding sweetened artificially
and one slice of bright orange yam.

She wants to be like everybody else, my mother.
She wants it all: two breasts, a real dessert,
a daughter whose white hair does not surprise her.
She wants to find the words to tell me she wants it all.
She wants to know who *they* are.

In the top drawer of a dresser she does not use,
my mother's prosthesis has a life of its own.
Neither jellyfish nor boob nor recyclable,
it lies in wait.

One day, my mother will find her breast,
and she will want to play catch with it
or dress it up like a baby doll or eat it with a spoon.
"Here," I'll say. "You'll want to drink your milk."

✳

REALITY RX

Ellen Morris Prewitt

Rx: Caution: Hallucinogenic. The Body Will Refuse To Mind

I am at the dentist's office under the influence of nitrous oxide, laughing gas. The dentist is performing a root canal, a low-class, white-trash operation as far as I'm concerned. "Use the rubber dam," the dentist tells the hygienist, and I taste bitter chalk. The procedure will remove the root and nerves, killing the tooth so it won't "rot". Then I'll need a crown so the tooth won't get brittle and break off. I've tried to avoid the whole disgusting mess, but the lazy, good-for-nothing tooth gave up the ghost, letting me down for good.

"Tooth," I say from inside the laughing gas. "You're dead to me."

My tooth, already sedated, doesn't respond.

Later, long after I've left the dentist's office, complications from the root canal will lead to an abscess which leads to oral surgery which leads to a night terror before the oral surgery which throws me off the bed and leads to an almost—but not—broken nose.

I swear: I'm a perfectly healthy individual.

Until my body decides to act otherwise.

It has a mind of its own.

Rx: Important: Do Not Crush Or Chew. Swallow Whole.

Once, when I broke my hand, they put me in an operating room and positioned a mirror so I could see what was going on.

I watched, awake, as they drilled a pin into the splitting skin, I watched as the long black rod disappeared into my unfeeling hand. I was interested, in an intellectual sort of way, as to what was happening. But my mind had no sympathy for my lifeless, antiseptic-swabbed hand.

When the mind wavers away from the body or the body scoots off without the mind, a crevice opens and you can wedge yourself in. This isn't the fogged reality of alcohol or psychedelic drugs or poisonous blow-fish. It's the reality that stands there all the time, but unseen. Like when the expensive lining of your good coat rips, and you can see the space behind. What's there may not be that interesting, but it's been hidden from view.

And now it's seen.

Rx: Take 1 Pill Every 6 Hrs Until Reality Disappears

Because we thought I had a kidney stone, my husband drove me to the doctor. To help with the pain, the doctor gave me Dilaudid. The drug did not touch the pain, but now I was throwing up. I threw up in the doctor's flower bed. In the middle of an intersection, my husband turning left, I hung my head out the car window and threw up. At the shopping center, in front of the drugstore, I got down on my hands and knees and threw up in the monkey grass. A kind woman stopped, asked, "Are you okay?" Kneeling there in the monkey grass, I tried to explain about my husband's being inside getting me a prescription, but I threw up.

I could've cared less, that it was the busiest intersection in town, that the shopping center was owned by my husband. I'd lost every inhibition I'd ever owned. The total need of my body—not the drugs—kicked me into this clarified spot.

The next day, I told my husband, "I was sick as a dog."

"I know, baby," he said. "I was there."

Rx: Warning: Induction of Non-Reality Can Become Addictive

Later that week, my aunt sent me a get-well card with a cartoon dog on the front. The dog was talking about being sick... as a dog.

Fame spreads.

If I were sick, really sick, I'd want what those who've been wrenched into illness want: their regular lives back. But my distress is run-of-the-mill, ordinary, and so I toy with world of the ill.

I am recuperating—from a virus, the flu, I don't know what—so I go to the hangout of the newly-recuperating: the Wal-Mart. There, the slightly-weak can walk the aisles, drifting, like physical TV. Each aisle, a new channel. Except better—you can buy things. Like potholders. And necklaces that say, "Spoiled." Like the time I recuperated at my grand-mother's house and lunch was brought in on a tray. I lolled, sinking deep-er and deeper into the sickness role. Until my then-husband said, "Get your butt out of bed and come home."

I held out for two more days.

Now, I wait for that time when mind and body are friends again, no longer at odds. When everyday reality returns. I hold out for health.

Or do I?

Rx: Take All Pills Even If You're Already Dead

My heart beats on the screen. We're checking to see if I have a condi-tion where your heart collapses into itself each time it pumps. The tech points to the motion that shows, yep, I'm collapsing.

The beating valve looks like an elf's foot. The little foot is kicking, kicking, every second I'm breathing. "Autonomic" they call it when the body keeps us alive without our mind having to instruct it.

I tear up in gratitude for the hard-working heart. I want to ask the tech if others cry at the sight of their determined hearts, but I don't know him that well.

When the test is done, the doctor calls me in for consultation. He reassures me: this bodily defect enhances the mind. Apparently, the col-lapsing valve correlates highly with intelligence and creativity. I nod, and the doctor yaks... and yaks. Finally, it dawns on me—this guy is hitting on me, in a pale wormy sort of way. I want to go back to the subject of my heart.

My friend Mable's heart stops beating at night. It used to scare her, when she woke up and her heart wasn't beating. Now, she's reconciled. "It starts again," she says.

RX: WHEN ALL PILLS ARE GONE, THROW AWAY THE BODY

It's an accommodation she's reached with her body, an understanding: if you'll keep it between the ditches, I'll ride along with you.

Until the ride ends, of course.

A woman I know spent a lot of money to get a breast reduction. "They grew back," she says. "That's where your body stores fat when you gain weight." Like a cartoonist's giant pencil had erased the breasts, but the determined body drew them back on, battling for Saturday morning supremacy.

When I do yoga, my mind separates from my body. "Rest, little foot," I say to the lapped-over, worn-out foot that lives at the end of my leg. Talking to the tired foot as if it were a fat little puppy who'd exhausted herself chasing her own tail. The yoga instructor would be appalled—we're supposed to be melding, not unmelding, body and mind.

Mind without body, body of mine.

Comes the end of time, there you are, on the hospital bed, your mind hovering at the ceiling, looking down on your lifeless body.

All the King's horses and all the King's men.

What shall we sing?

Silence enters, the world without end.

Amen.

Contributors' Notes

DeeDee Agee, daughter of the late novelist and film critic, James Agee, is a writer currently at work on a memoir about growing up in Greenwich Village in the fifties and sixties. She has an MFA in writing from Columbia School of the Arts and has taught writing in area colleges as well as privately for many years. Agee has also worked as a waitress, house painter, reproductive counselor, chef, and software trainer at the United Nations. She is currently a member of the Writers' Room of Boston and has done readings with them as well as at Arlington Street Church in Boston. She lives in Hingham, Massachusetts, with her husband, Paul Sprecher, who is trustee of the James Agee Trust.

Askhari writes because she can. Her work has appeared in *Essence*, *Black Issues Book Reviews*, *Class*, *Catalyst*, *Rap Pages*, and *Urban Profile Magazines*. She has written and reported for the Afro-American newspapers in Washington, DC, and in Baltimore, Maryland. Her poetry, fiction, and non-fiction have appeared in various publications including *In the Tradition*, *Testimony*, *Sex & the Single Girl*, and *Role Call*.

Julie Auer is a lawyer and freelance writer. She has published two mystery novels as well as short fiction and essays. She lives in Knoxville.

Sara Baker earned an MA in English and Creative Writing from the University of Tennessee. Her writing has been published in *We'Moon* and *Earth's Daughters*, and she won the John C. Hodges Excellence in Poetry Award in 2003. She has led workshops at numerous conferences and was part of the UT's Writers in the Library series in 2004. She works as a copywriter in Knoxville.

Janée J. Baugher holds a BS in Human Anatomy/Physiology from Boston University and an MFA in Poetry from Eastern Washington University. Dozens of her poems have appeared in anthologies and journals, some have been adapted for the stage (dance and music), and she's a recent Pushcart prize nominee. She teaches at the University of Washington Experimental College in Seattle during the academic year and at Interlochen Center for the Arts (Michigan) each summer, where she's the summer director of the creative writing program.

Linda R. Bell is an accomplished free-lance writer and photographer with over 125 individual poems published in over 50 literary journals and one nominated for a Pushcart prize. In addition to poetry, Bell has published nature and health nonfiction in over a dozen magazines. She has garnered regional and national awards for her poetry and photography. Her book, *The Red Butterfly: Lupus Patients Can Survive*, was published in 1983; the sequel, *What I Remember: Lessons from a Lupus Patient*, is forthcoming in 2007. Bell has had systematic lupus for 30 years. She lives in Knoxville, Tennessee, with her cat, Kipling.

Margery Weber Bensey lives in a historic house in Park City with her husband Michael Bensey and their son Kiernan. She holds an MA in Literature from the University of Tennessee, where she has served as a writer, editor, researcher, and writing teacher over the past 25 years. She currently is editor of *Blackberry Corner*, *The Inkwell*, and *Staff Stuff*, and history columnist for *The Parkridge Press*, and maintains related websites. Her academic and historic research and writing have appeared in *Assessment Update*, *Breathing the Same Air*, *HomeWorks: A Book of Tennessee Writers*, and Park City. "The Youth" was written during her art student days.

Carole Borges, author of *Disciplining the Devil's County* published by Alice James Books, was raised aboard a schooner on the Mississippi River in the 1950s. She learned the art of storytelling from the fishermen and river folk she met along the way and also from the river itself—the stories it whispered and the lessons it taught. Carole lives in Knoxville, Tennessee, with her white cat and spends most of her time writing or playing in her garden. Her poems have appeared in *Poetry*, *Bardsong*, *Soundings East*, *Cimmaron Review* and many others. Her essays and newspaper articles have been published in a variety of periodicals, including *The North Shore Sunday*, *The Lynn Item*, *The Westside Gazette*, *The Change Agent*, and *Rudder Magazine*.

Gaylord Brewer is a professor at Middle Tennessee State University, where he edits *Poems & Plays*. His most recent book of poetry, a collection of apologias, is *Let Me Explain* (Iris Press 2006). His work also appears in Best American Poetry 2006.

Rebecca Brooks lives in Oak Ridge and teaches writing at Pellissippi Community College, Roane State, Tennessee Tech University, and for the Tennessee Board of Regent's online degree program. She holds a BA in Political Science and an MA in English, both from the University of Tennessee. She has had stories published in *The Louisville Review*, *The Hawai'i Review*, *The Birmingham Arts Review*, and in the Knoxville Writers' Guild's *Migrants and Stowaways*. She has completed a novel and is looking for a publisher and is working on a second novel. She has three grown children and two grandchildren.

Bill Brown, who grew up in Dyersburg, Tennessee, is the author of four collections of poetry, a writing text on which he collaborated with Malcolm Glass, and the new chapbook, *Yesterday's Hay*. During the past twenty years, he has published hundreds of poems and articles in college journals, magazines and anthologies. In 1999 Brown wrote and co-produced the Instructional Television Series, *Student Centered Learning*, for Nashville Public Television. He holds a degree in history from Bethel College and graduate degrees in English from the Bread Loaf School of English, Middlebury College and George Peabody College. Since 1983, Brown directed the writing program at Hume-Fogg Academic High School in Nashville. He retired from Hume-Fogg in May, 2003, and accepted a part time lecturer's position at Peabody College of Vanderbilt University. In 1995 the National Foundation for Advancement in the Arts named him Distinguished Teacher in the Arts. He has been a Scholar in Poetry at the Bread Loaf Writers Conference, a Fellow at the Virginia Center for the Creative Arts, a two-time recipient of Fellowships in poetry from the Tennessee Arts Commission, and twice the recipient of the Smith-Corona Award for entering the best student writing in the National Scholastic Writing Awards. He and his wife Suzanne live in the hills of Robertson County with the ghost of their old cat, Soliloquy. Brown has new work forthcoming in *Slant, Karamu, Tar River Poetry, Poem, The English Journal, Eclipse, The North American Review, CrossRoads,* and *The Monchilla Review.*

Jeannette Brown has a master's degree in urban studies. Her work experience includes publicity for theatre, dance, and other arts groups, as well as writing copy for an ad agency. Her work has been published in *Southwestern Literary Review, The Texas Observer, ArtSpace, Mother Earth, Breathing the Same Air—An East Tennessee Anthology, Suddenly IV, Bellevue Literary Review,* and other publications. She is the editor of *Literary Lunch,* a food anthology.

Hannah Cook grew up in Illinois and Kentucky and now is a PhD student in poetry at the University of Tennessee. Her poems have appeared in journals such as *Poetry Midwest, Pegasus, The Chaffin Journal,* and *Kudzu,* and in the 2004 anthology *Poetry as Prayer: Appalachian Women Speak* from Wind Publications.

Cindy Childress was awarded the 2005 Marcella Siegel Memorial Poetry Award for her poem, "Spontaneous Generation of a Dappled Thing," and her work has been recently published in *Altar Magazine, Southern Hum, The Southwestern Review,* and *The Red Booth Review.* In June she presented her poetry at the National Women's Studies Association Conference in Oakland, California. She teaches writing and literature courses at the University of Louisiana at Lafayette where she is working on a PhD in English with emphases on literary theory, women's literature, and creative writing.

Susan Deer Cloud (Eastern Blackfoot, Seneca, Mohawk) is an award-winning writer with poems published in such places as *Rosebud, Mid-American Review, Prairie Schooner, Ms.,* the multi-cultural anthology *Unsettling America* and the Native anthology *Sister Nations.* She is the editor of the anthology *Confluence* and of three books of poetry. Deer Cloud has also received a New York State Foundation of the Arts Fellowship. She likes to shine with sunsets over Susquehanna and Chenango Rivers, to hold Underground Poets Readings in Binghamton, New York, and to play with her cats in her garrets.

Donna Doyle was born in Knoxville, Tennessee, and raised in Seymour, Tennessee. Her poetry has received numerous awards including the Libba Moore Gray Poetry Prize, the Robert Burns/Terry Semple Award, the New Millennium Writings Poetry Prize, and the Tennessee Mountain Writers Poetry Award. *Low Explosions* marks her fifth Knoxville Writers' Guild publication. Doyle resides in Knoxville.

Emily Dziuban edited *Migrants & Stowaways*, the Knoxville Writers' Guild's 2004 anthology. She holds a BA in English from Winthrop University in South Carolina and an MA in English from the University of Tennessee, where she currently teaches writing and literature classes. She has won John C. Hodges awards for her writing, teaching and tutoring. The University of New Orleans also awarded her a runner-up prize for her fiction.

Rebecca Efroymson resides in Oak Ridge, Tennessee, where she is an environmental scientist at Oak Ridge National Laboratory. She won first place in the Knoxville Writers' Guild's Leslie Garrett fiction contest in 1999. "Moving through Oz" is her first foray into the memoir and creative nonfiction genres and her first published literary piece.

Raised in eastern Kentucky where the traditions of home and hearth are still the first lessons of little girls, **Sydney England** learned the beauty of a well-placed word early and still thrills at finding one. Thus, it was kismet that she ended up editing *The Pikeville Review*, the literary magazine published yearly by the humanities division of Pikeville College. After completing a stint as a full time at-home mom, she earned a BS in Middle School Education with a second major in English and an MA in English. She teaches at Pikeville College and lives in Pikeville, Kentucky, with her husband, Tommy, where they are invaded often by their three grown children and three grandchildren.

Christine Omodi-Engola is a graduate student in English at The University of Tennessee. A recent transplant to Knoxville, Omodi-Engola has spent most of her time being educated in the northeast. In addition to being a writer she is also an actress, having recently performed in the stage version of *The Exonerated*.

Kelly Falzone is a poet, teaching artist, and counselor living in Nashville. She has been awarded poetry prizes from the Tennessee Writers Alliance, the Knoxville Writers' Guild, and the Chester H. Jones Foundation, as well as nominated for the esteemed Pushcart Prize. Her work was a finalist in both The Nation's 1994 "Discovery" contest and the 2006 Berry College Emerging Women Writers Competition. Kelly's poetry has appeared in anthologies and journals such as *Clackamas Literary Review*, *Cumberland Poetry Review*, *Poets On:*, and the *Journal of Poetry Therapy*, as well as been featured on the stage in Nashville and Atlanta. A member of both the Key West Writers' Workshops and The Community of Writers at Squaw Valley, she has studied under the guidance of such master poets as Sharon Olds, Lucille Clifton, and Kate Daniels. Through her company, Poet People, Kelly facilitates "Swim With Words," creative writing workshops for youth and adults throughout the Nashville community. More about Kelly can be found at www.poetpeople.net.

Leslye Stewart Ford recently graduated from the University of Tennessee with an MA in English.

Katherine Frank is an Assistant Professor in the Language and Literature Division, Hiwassee College, Madisonville, Tennessee. She is also the Resident Director of Brock Hall, a women's residence hall at Hiwassee College, where she lives with husband Kim and daughter Zoe. She only shares her Mama Heat with immediate family members.

Kim Frank teaches composition and literature classes at Tennessee Wesleyan College in Athens, Tennessee. He lives in Madisonville, Tennessee, where he has cultivated lifelong bad habits.

Alice Friman is the author of seven collections of poetry, most recently *Zoo* (Arkansas 1999), winner of the Ezra Pound Poetry Award from Truman State University and the Sheila Margaret Motton Prize from the New England Poetry Club, and *Inverted Fire* (BkMk 1997, rpt. 1998). An eighth book, *The Book of the Rotten Daughter*, is forthcoming from BkMk Press in 2006. Her poems appear in *Poetry*, *The Georgia Review*, *Boulevard*, *The Southern Review*, *The Gettysburg Review*, and *Shenandoah*, which awarded Friman the 2002 James Boatwright III Prize for Poetry. She has received fellowships from the Indiana Arts Commission and the Arts Council of Indianapolis and has been awarded residencies at many colonies including MacDowell and Yaddo. She was named Writer in Residence at Bernheim Arboretum and Research Forest in 2003-04. She has won three prizes from Poetry Society of America and in 2001-02 was named to the Georgia Poetry Circuit. Professor Emerita at the University of Indianapolis, Friman now lives in Milledgeville, Georgia, where she is Instructor of Creative Writing and Poetry and poetry editor of *Arts & Letters*.

Rebekah Goemaat is a native of rural Iowa. She moved to Knoxville, Tennessee, in 1991 and later graduated from the University of Tennessee with a bachelor's degree in social work. She has served as a social services case manager, a program director, a preschool teacher and a therapeutic foster parent. She currently directs an Early Childhood Education program. When she is not at work or writing, she enjoys playing guitar, skating and doing most anything with her son, Andrew.

Jesse Graves is a native of East Tennessee and is currently working toward a PhD in English at The University of Tennessee. He received a BA from UT and an MFA from Cornell University, and his poems are forthcoming in *New Millennium Writings* and *CrossRoads: A Southern Culture Annual*. He won first place in the 1997 Knoxville Writers' Guild Libba Moore Gray Poetry Contest, and second place in 2005. He lives in North Knoxville with his wife Lisa, his daughter Chloe, and Chloe's golden retriever, Loie.

Connie Jordan Green lives on a farm in Loudon County, where she writes a newspaper column, novels for young people, and poetry. She speaks frequently at schools and workshops. Her hobbies include gardening, knitting, reading, and playing with her seven grandchildren.

Judy Lee Green is an award-winning writer and spoken-word artist. She has been recognized throughout the Southeast for her work by the Appalachian Writers Association, the Tennessee Mountain Writers, The Alabama Writers' Conclave, and other organizations. She has been published in literary journals, magazines, newspapers, trade publications, and on the Web. Her most recent works have appeared in *Southern Arts Journal*, *Birmingham Arts Journal*, *Now and Then: The Appalachian Magazine*, and *The Rambler*. She began writing at the age of nine and has passed the passion to her daughter, Kory Wells (also in this anthology). Currently residing in Murfreesboro, Tennessee, she is compiling a collection of creative nonfiction about her childhood, growing up in East Tennessee in the 1950s. Email her at JudyLeeGreen@bellsouth.net.

Brian Griffin holds an MFA in Creative Writing from the University of Virginia. His fiction and poetry appears in a number of literary journals, including *Shenandoah*, *Mississippi Review*, *New Millennium Writings*, *Asheville Poetry Review*, *Southern Poetry Review*, *Snake Nation Review*, *Clockwatch Review*, *New Delta Review*, *The Distillery*, and elsewhere. He received the Mary McCarthy Award for Short Fiction for his collection Sparkman in the Sky and Other Stories.

Jay N. Helmstutler is currently a student in the MFA program in creative writing at American University in Washington, DC. He works as a paralegal by day and writes by night. He is working on his first collection of short stories.

L.A. Hoffer is a PhD candidate in creative writing at the University of Tennessee, currently completing a novel set in the twin towns of Bristol, Tennessee, and Bristol, Virginia. Her fiction has appeared in *Blue Mesa Review* and is forthcoming in *Stories from the Blue Moon Café*.

Elizabeth Howard has an MA in English from Vanderbilt University. She writes both poetry and fiction. Her work has been published in *Xavier*

Review, *Cold Mountain Review*, *Comstock Review*, *Wind*, *Poem*, *Appalachian Heritage*, *The Licking River Review*, *Big Muddy*, and other journals. She has two books of poetry: *Anemones* (Grandmother Earth 1998) and *Gleaners* (Grandmother Earth 2005).

Frank Jamison is a graduate of Union University and the University of Tennessee. His first book of poems, *Marginal Notes*, was published in 2001. His poetry, essays and children's stories have won numerous prizes. His poems have appeared recently in *Nimrod*, *Fox Cry*, *Poem*, *Red Wheelbarrow*, *Sanskrit*, *The Tennessee English Journal* and *Illuminations*. He was the 2004 winner of the Robert Burns/Terry Semple Memorial Poetry Prize and the 2005 winner of the Libba Moore Gray Poetry Prize. He is a member of the Knoxville Writers' Guild and the Tennessee Writers Alliance. He lives and writes in Roane County, Tennessee.

Jessie L. Janeshek is a student in the University of Tennessee's PhD in English with Creative Dissertation program. A West Virginia native, she holds an MFA in Poetry from Emerson College, Boston. Her work has appeared in *The Sow's Ear Poetry Review*, *Washington Square*, and *Passages North*.

Edison Jennings earned a BA in English Literature while serving active duty in the US Navy. He received an honorable discharge and later earned an MFA from the Warren Wilson Program for Writers. In 2005, he was awarded a Tennessee Williams Scholarship at Sewanee. Jennings serves on the English faculty and directs the writing center at Virginia Intermont College. His poems have appeared in *Blue Fifth Review*, *Boulevard*, *The Kenyon Review*, *Nantahala Review*, *The Nebraska Review*, *Poetry Daily*, *River Styx*, *Southern Cultures*, *Southern Poetry Review*, and other journals.

Stephanie N. Johnson was born in Minnesota but has lived in Alaska and Thailand. She holds a BA from the University of Alaska and an MFA in Creative Writing from the University of Minnesota. Her poetry and nonfiction has appeared in *AGNI*, *Borderlands*, and *Dislocate*. She is currently working on a memoir about hunting, archery, and aviation.

Libby Falk Jones is professor of English at Berea College, where she teaches courses in creative, academic, and professional writing. Her poems and essays have been published in regional and national journals and anthologies, including *Writing on the Edge, New Millennium Writings, Coffee Talk Quarterly, Kudzu, Heartstone, Heartland, Poetry As Prayer: Appalachian Women Speak,* and *I to I: Life Writing by Kentucky Feminists.* She is currently at work on a full-length memoir and two books of poems.

David E. Joyner, artist and illustrator, is a retired member of the conceptual staff of the Tennessee Valley Authority's Architectural Design Branch. He started writing short stories at the age of sixty-five and refers to himself as "an old man but a young writer." His fiction and poetry have appeared in *New Millennium Writings,* and in the Knoxville Writers' Guild's anthologies *Literary Lunch* and *Migrants and Stowaways,* and the Knoxville-based anthology, *Knoxville Bound.*

Chimena Kabasenche grew up in Nashville and lives in Knoxville with her own family. Though relocating with her family is inevitable, she considers Tennessee her home.

Marilyn Kallet is the author of 12 books, including *Circe, After Hours,* poetry from BkMk Press/UMKC, and *The Art of College Teaching: 28 Takes* (U of Tennessee Press 2005). Commonwealth Books of Boston will publish a new edition of her translations of Paul Eluard's Last Love Poems under their Black Widow Press imprint in 2006. Kallet is the poetry editor of New Millennium Writings and was inducted into the East Tennessee Literary Hall of Fame in poetry in 2005. She is a professor of English at the University of Tennessee, where she directed the creative writing program from 1986-2003.

Gabby Kindell is a graduate student in English with an emphasis in creative writing at the University of Tennessee. She has previously published in *The Louisville Review* and *Inscape.* She tries to be an activist. Her heart is in the South.

Margrethe Krogh earned a BA in English, with a concentration in creative writing, from The University of Tennessee. Krogh is originally from Washington, DC, and currently lives in Sevierville with her three children and twelve cats

Born in Snowflake, Virginia, **Judy Loest** earned an MA in English from the University of Tennessee in 1998. Her awards include the 2004 James Still Poetry Award and the 2004 Olay/Poetry Society of America Fine Lines Poetry Contest. Her work has appeared in *Now & Then*, *The Cortland Review*, *New Millennium Writings*, *Crossroads: A Southern Culture Annual*, and on buses and subways in St. Paul/Minneapolis as part of PSA's Poetry in Motion program. She has also published travel writing in *France Magazine* and is editor of *Knoxville Bound* (2004), a literary anthology inspired by Knoxville, Tennessee.

Beth Long lives in Knoxville, Tennessee where her life is graced by her husband John, daughter Anna, four cats, and a parrotlet.

Linda Parsons Marion is the poetry editor of *Now & Then* magazine and the author of *Home Fires*. Her work has appeared widely, including *The Georgia Review*, *Shenandoah*, *Iowa Review*, *Asheville Poetry Review*, and *Prairie Schooner*. One of her poems was nominated for a 2006 Pushcart Prize, and she has received two literary fellowships from the Tennessee Arts Commission, among other awards. Essays, poems, and interviews have appeared in *Listen Here: Women Writing in Appalachia* (U Press of Kentucky 2003) and *Her Words: Diverse Voices in Contemporary Appalachian Women's Poetry* (U of Tennessee Press 2002), and *Sleeping with One Eye Open: Women Writers and the Art of Survival* (U of Georgia Press 1999). Marion is an editor at the University of Tennessee. You can most often find her digging in her North Hills gardens or out and about with her husband, poet Jeff Daniel Marion.

Laura McCoy is a native Knoxvillian and paralegal graduate of Pellissippi State. In addition to writing poems and short stories, she enjoys the outdoors, loves whitewater rafting, and occasionally tries to make pleasant sounds with her guitar.

Jeanne McDonald has published a novel, *Water Dreams*, and is co-author of two nonfiction books written with her husband, Fred Brown's *The Serpent Handlers*, and *Growing Up Southern*. She has also published short fiction, reviews and articles in anthologies, magazines, newspapers and journals. She is a recipient of the Tennessee Arts Commission/Alex Haley Fiction Fellowship, a Washington Prize in Fiction, and awards for the novel from the National League of American Pen Women and the National Writers' Association. Now retired from an editorial position at the University of Tennessee, she lives in Knoxville and is a freelance writer and a contributing writer for *Metro Pulse* and *Knoxville Magazine*.

Liz McGeachy lives in Norris, Tennessee, where she is a free-lance writer of poetry, essays, articles, and a weekly column on small-town life for the *Clinton Courier News*. Her poems have been published in *Amherst Review*, *Appalachian Heritage*, *Sanskrit*, and other journals, and she won the Robert Burns Poetry Contest in 2004. In addition to writing, she performs traditional and folk music with her husband, Tim Marema, under the name Liz&Tim, and enjoys jumping on the trampoline with her two kids, Walker and Graham, and their dog.

Stephen Mead is a published writer/artist living in New York. Some of his merchandise can be found at www.cafepress.com/stephenmeadart, http://www.lulu.com/stephenmead, and www.absolutearts.com/portfolios/s/stephenmead.

Kali Meister is an actress, performance poet, playwright, and nonfiction writer. Her poetry has been featured in *Circle Magazine*, *Prism*, *Pegasus Review*, and *New Millennium Writings*. She was the 2005 winner of the University of Tennessee's Margaret Atley Woodruff for fiction and the 2006 winner for playwright. She was also the recipient of the 2005 and 2006 Eleanor Burke nonfiction award through the University of Tennessee. She is currently on the Board of Speakers for the Knoxville Writers' Guild and performed her original play *Exposed* for the Writers' Guild in March 2006.

A native of Johnson City, Tennessee, **Terri Beth Miller** earned her BA in English at Tusculum College before relocating to Charlottesville, Virginia, to complete a master's degree in literature at the University of Virginia. Currently, Miller is pursuing her doctorate at the University of Tennessee, Knoxville, where she specializes in modern and postmodern literature and cultural studies. Her scholarly work has appeared in various academic journals. This is the first publication of her creative writing.

Felicia Mitchell lives in rural Washington County, Virginia, and teaches English at Emory & Henry College. Her poems have appeared in a variety of journals and anthologies over the years, recently in *PMS poemmemoirstory*, *Earth's Daughters*, *Rough Places Plain*, and *Poems of the Mountains* (edited by Margot Wizansky for Salt Marsh Pottery Press). *Earthenware Fertility Figure*, a chapbook, won first place and was published by Talent House Press in Oregon. In her community, Felicia writes a weekly column for the *Washington County News*.

Andrew Najberg lives in Knoxville, Tennessee. He received his BA and MA in English from The University of Tennessee at Knoxville. His work is forthcoming in *New Millennium Writings* and *Bat City Review*, and his poetry has won the John C. Hodges Prize in poetry.

Natalia Nazarewicz is a senior at Oak Ridge High School. She will attend Brown University in the fall of 2006.

Billie Nelson was born and raised in Maryville. She began her academic career at Pellissippi State Technical Community College, where she graduated with an associate of arts degree in Spring 2003. At that time, she was the first student to graduate using the University of Tennessee articulation agreement for creative writing. Billie transferred to the University of Tennessee, Knoxville, in Fall 2003. Billie is currently pursing an Honors English degree in creative writing, and she plans to graduate in 2006. She received the Margaret Woodruff Writing Award in Spring 2006. She desires to obtain an MFA in creative writing. Her main goal is to become like the teachers who provided the sparks, kindling, and logs that initiated and fueled her desire to write.

Kay Newton lives in the 4th & Gill Historic District of Knoxville, where she is working on a novel. She also writes stories, poems, songs, plays, articles, and other forms. Among the highest honors her writing has received is being included in all the KWG anthologies published so far (but not the book of the memoirs, since Kay's too young to write her memoirs yet—nor is she old enough to qualify "at risk" for flu, despite the implications of the poem included here). She hopes the anthologies will keep coming out, and that her work will continue to be included.

Delilah Ferne O'Haynes, EdD, is of Irish and Cherokee heritage and the daughter of a coal miner. She grew up in Clintwood, Virginia, and has resided all her life in the Appalachian region, receiving her doctorate at the University of Tennessee, and teaching in Virginia, Tennessee, North Carolina, Georgia, and now West Virginia. She has been in Who's Who, both as a student and a teacher, and was honored in Prestige International Who's Who Registry of Outstanding Professionals, 2006-2007. O'Haynes currently teaches creative writing at Concord University in Athens, West Virginia. She is a widely published and celebrated author of fiction, non-fiction, and poetry, with educational and literary articles in journals such as *Tennessee English Journal* and *Tennessee Philological Bulletin*; poetry in many recognized publications, such as *The Sow's Ear* and *The American Indian Culture and Research Journal of UCLA*; and Appalachian fiction in publications such as *Potato Eyes* and *Potomac Review*. Her first book is an artistic collaboration of poetry and photography entitled *The Character of Mountains*, which can be obtained from www.appalachianauthorsguild.com. A survivor of rape, abuse, and cancer, O'Haynes now devotes much of her time to helping other victims become survivors through her books and workshops on journaling to healing, poetry therapy, overcoming violence, reclaiming Native heritage, and surviving cancer. Future books include *Walk Free from Fear of Cancer*; *Rise, Woman, Rise*; *From Fearful to Fearless: Real Stories, Real People*; *Fearless Woman*; *Fearless: Strategies for Overcoming Fear*; and *Glorious Woman*.

William Orem's first novel-in-stories, *Zombi, You My Love*, won the New Writers Award from the Great Lakes Colleges Association, formerly given to Lousie Erdrich, Sherman Alexie, Alice Munro, Richard Ford and others. His poetry and short fiction have been in over fifty journals, including *Alaska Quarterly Review* and *Sou'wester*, and he has twice been nominated for the Puschart Prize. He works as science editor at Science and Theology News in Boston and is seeking representation.

Katie O'Sullivan is married, lives in Houston, Texas, and has always loved to write but started submitting work only in the last four years. O'Sullivan has lived in China, Lebanon, Libya, the Netherlands and of course, the United States. Her poems have appeared in *Promise Magazine*, *Texas Poetry Calendar* (2004 and 2005), *Cup of Comfort* (poem and memoir), and *Noble Generation II*, a monologue produced by Fan Factory Theatre, Houston

Jo Ann Pantanizopoulos can smell her way around. Acutely disposed to sniffing out the truth in pungent spices, fresh oregano, nasty diapers, and homemade lemoncello, she has published Greek lullaby translations in *Two Lins*, as well as several articles on young adult literature, poetry translation in the high school English class and word play in various state English journals. Her work has also appeared in *Breathing the Same Air*, *Literary Lunch*, and *Migrants and Stowaways*. Pantanizopoulos recently won an award of excellence for her poem, "Sunday Afternoon," in the 2003 Terry Semple Memorial Poetry Contest. In addition to her job as an administrator at Pellissippi State Technical Community College, she maintains websites for the Knoxville Writers' Guild, Pellissippi State, Celtic Cat Publishing, and others.

Christine Parkhurst is a teacher and writer who divides her time between Knoxville, Tennessee, and Danville, California. She loves children, dogs, her husband, art, music, movies, writing, gardening, and dancing—though not necessarily in that order.

Since receiving her MFA in Creative Writing from Emerson College, **Charlotte Pence** has been teaching at Belmont University in Nashville, Tennessee. Her poetry has appeared in a variety of journals including *Southern Poetry Review*, *Seattle Review*, and *The Spoon River Poetry Review*. In 2003, she received the individual artist fellowship in poetry from the Tennessee Arts Commission and the New Millennium Writing Award for Poetry, XVI, 2004. In the fall of 2006, she will enter the PhD program in English at the University of Tennessee, Knoxville.

Debra A. Poole is a native of Murray, Kentucky, and a graduate of the University of Tennessee College of Law. She has published professional articles on charitable giving in *Planned Giving Today*, *PG Mentor*, and *Planned Giving Plainly*. Her humor and poetry has appeared in *New Millennium Writings* (2005-2006), *Migrants and Stowaways* (2004), and *Senior Living*.

Excerpts from **Ellen Morris Prewitt's** memoir, *Snow Melts Either Way*, have appeared or are forthcoming in the *Alaska Quarterly Review*, *North Dakota Quarterly*, and *River Teeth*. Other nonfiction has been, or will be, in *Fourth Genre*, *Texas Review*, *Barrelhouse Magazine*, *Brevity*, *Strut*, *The Rambler*, *Skirt!*, and elsewhere. She was the nonfiction Peter Taylor Fellow at the Kenyon Summer Writing Program in 2005. Her commentaries have aired on public radio for five years; one of the commentaries won a PRNDI from NPR.

Candance W. Reaves is a freelance writer living on a farm in Blount County at the foot of Chilhowee Mountain with her husband, John, a writer and English professor. She has published in three previous KWG anthologies: *Voices from the Valley*, *All Around Us: Poems from the Valley* (co-edited with Linda Parsons Marion), and *Breathing the Same Air*. She has also published in *New Millennium Writings*, *Homeworks: A Book of Tennessee Writers* and was a historical travel writer for *Appalachian Life* magazine.

Joe Rector has taught high school English for twenty-nine years. He also writes a column for *The Fountain City Focus*, *The Knoxville News Sentinel*, and *The Oak Ridge Observer*. His work has appeared in *Chicken Soup for the Mother and Son Soul* and *Grandparent Magazine*. Presently, he is finishing a book-length manuscript titled The Common is Spectacular.

Ronda Redden Reitz graduated from the Western College of Miami University (Ohio) in 1979 and received her PhD from the University of Tennessee in 1998. An occasional poet and sometime lecturer for the UT Psychology department, she is a clinical psychologist in private practice in Knoxville, Tennessee.

Richard Remine's photographs were a part of the KWG anthology *Breathing the Same Air* and were published in several issues of *New Millennium Writings*, and other literary journals. His photography has been exhibited locally, regionally, and nationally. For seven years he was the instructor in photography and black and white film printing at the Knoxville Arts and Fine Crafts Center. Richard was educated in Communications at the University of Tennessee and for the past seventeen years has been an actor in many productions for a variety of area theatrical groups and regional commercials.

Jack Rentfro's prose and poetry has appeared in the past four Knoxville Writers' Guild anthologies. Among other honors, he has won the Leslie Garrett Short Story Award (2006) and the Tennessee Mountain Writers' Conference short story competition (1993). His greatest pleasure as a writer and editor came from a labor-of-love project, *Cumberland Avenue Revisited: Four Decades of Music from Knoxville, Tennessee* (Cardinal Publishing 2003), an anthology combining his interests in music and writing. A native of Cleveland, Tennessee, Rentfro has lived in Knoxville since 1971 when he began working on a 10-year bachelor's degree program at the University of Tennessee. The freelance writer and editor's spoken word musical combo appears sporadically around town. He and his wife, Angie, raise vegetables, culinary herbs (which he occasionally sells at the Market Square Farmers' Market) and take in stray animals at their small farm just a pinecone toss south of the Union county line.

Sara Roberts, a native Knoxvillian, is a freshman majoring in English at the University of Tennessee, Knoxville. This is her first published poem.

Curt Rode has appeared into two previous KWG anthologies, *Migrants and Stowaways* and *Breathing the Same Air*. Other poems have appeared or are forthcoming in *The Sun*, *Florida Review*, *Sycamore Review*, and *Iron Horse Literary Review*. He received his PhD from the University of Tennessee in 1998. He now teaches creative writing and American literature at Texas Christian University, where he is also the poetry editor of *descant*.

Christopher Roethle received his BA in Creative Writing from the University of Tennessee, Knoxville, in 2005. He is currently enrolled in the MFA program at the University of Oregon, where he teaches introductory poetry writing.

Sheryl Hill Sallie was born and raised in East Knoxville. She holds a BS in Education from Knoxville College and an MS in Educational Psychology from The University of Tennessee. She won first place in the Tennessee Writers Alliance 1994 Poetry Competition. In 2001, she won an award of excellence in the Robert Burns Poetry Award. After 35 years of teaching in the Knoxville city and county school systems, she retired in December of 2004. She enjoys cooking, painting, and learning new things. She resides in Karns with her husband Reginald and their dog B.B.

Alicia Benjamin-Samuels was born in Washington, DC, and raised in the Wilmington, Delaware, area. She is an actor, director and poet. She studied theatre at Hunter College in New York City, at the Harlem Theatre Company and at Bushfire Theatre in Philadelphia. Her poems have appeared in London's *X Magazine*, *Black Arts Quarterly*, *WarpLand*, Philadelphia's *Open City: A Journal of Community Arts and Culture*, Yale University's *Black Ivy*, and the Web 'zines: *The Eintouist*, *SeeingBlack.com*, and *The New Verse News*. Her poem "The Way of a Lover" was featured in Londonart.co.uk's 2005 Art of Love exhibit. She resides in Nashville, Tennessee, with her husband and daughter.

Jane Sasser's work has appeared in *The Atlanta Review*, *The North American Review*, *The National Forum*, *Sow's Ear*, *RE:AL*, *ByLine*, *The Mid-America Poetry Review*, *Snowy Egret*, *Small Pond*, *The North Carolina Literary Review*, and numerous other publications. A high school teacher of English literature, American literature, and creative writing, she lives in Oak Ridge, Tennessee.

Deborah Scaperoth's work has appeared in various literary journals and anthologies including *New Millennium Writings*, *Yemassee*, *Number One*, *Migrants and Stowaways*, and *Knoxville Bound*.

Christina Schneider is from the entire United States, the byproduct of moving constantly during her formative years. She is a pre-med/psychology major at the University of Tennessee, Knoxville, and began in fiction by telling strangers in supermarkets rambling—often scandalous—stories about her kindergarten classmates, but she just started writing poetry this past year. This is her first publication.

Lucy Sieger is a freelance writer specializing in essays, features and profiles. She's published in *Metro Pulse*, *EvaMag*, *Knoxville News-Sentinel*, and *Southern Living*. She especially enjoys writing personal essays about the mundane yet illuminating stuff of daily life. She lives in Knoxville, Tennessee, with her husband, Mark, and their two canine babies, Jasper and Daisy.

Maureen A. Sherbondy has been published in *Carolina Woman* and *Phoebe* (SUNY, Oneonta). Her stories have been recognized as finalists in contests, including The Greensboro Awards, Writers' Workshop of Asheville, and Fish Publishing's one-page story contest. As a winner of the Piccolo Spoleto Fiction Open, Sherbondy recently read a story in Charleston at the Piccolo Spoleto Festival. Her novella, *Someone Drowning*, is a finalist in the William Faulkner–William Wisdom Creative Writing Competition (novella category). She resides in Raleigh, North Carolina, with her husband and three sons.

Arthur Smith's most recent books of poems are *The Late World* (2002) and *Orders of Affection* (1996), both from Carnegie Mellon University Press. Other new poems are forthcoming in *TriQuarterly*, *Poetry Miscellany*, and *Poetry International*. He is a professor of English at the University of Tennessee.

Heather Joyner Spica returned to Tennessee in 1997 after earning an MFA in Creative Writing from Sarah Lawrence College. Following an eight-year period of work as a librarian, teacher, and bi-weekly art critic/columnist for Knoxville's newspaper *Metro Pulse*, she is now devoting her time to her toddler son, Paolo, and his father, Mac. Her "Elemental Sestina" was written in response to specific words provided by her husband as a creative challenge-of-sorts.

Ellen Dennis Stein was born in Baltimore, raised in Maryland and DC, lived for 13 years on Martha's Vineyard, graduated from Wellesley College at the age of 43, and then went to law school in Boston. She returned to the city of her birth for eight years, moved west and now lives in the San Francisco Bay area. Denny works as an educational advocate for children with special needs, and volunteers with several child focused organizations. She studied with Frank Bidart, Cathy Hankla, Kendra Kopelke, and Charlotte Morgan; she writes poems, memoir, and essays. Denny has attended Nimrod Writers' Workshops since 1999. Her creative interests include photography, knitting, and laundry. She has published work in *Lumina*, *Welter*, and *Streetlight*. Denny is currently trying to find time to finish a book of letters between her grandmother and Gertrude Stein.

Laura Still lives in Knoxville with her two sons. Her day jobs include part-time dental hygienist, customer service at Vagabondia on Market Square, and USTA-certified tennis umpire. She is assistant poetry editor for *New Millennium Writings* and a member of the Knoxville Writers' Guild. She served as Treasurer for three years and currently administers the Young Writers' Poetry Prize. She has screened novels for the Peter Taylor Prize since its inception, and received the coveted Golden Shovel Award in 2005. Her recent publications include *Breathing the Same Air*, *Literary Lunch*,

Migrants and Stowaways, *Knoxville Bound*, *Knoxville News-Sentinel*, and *New Millennium Writings*. Other activities include tennis, strength training, and writing plays for the children's drama workshop at Church Street United Methodist Church, where she teaches grades 1 through 5. She was an assistant stage manager for Shakespeare on The Square for the summer in 2005 and stage manager for the Tennessee Stage Company's production of *The Foreigner* in November 2005.

Pam Strickland is a native of Harriman, Tennessee. "Interlude: Reading Virginia Woolf" was written originally a diversion from her master's thesis in rhetoric and composition at the University of Arkansas at Little Rock. Her creative nonfiction essays have appeared in *The East Tennessee Writer*, the *Arkansas Hunger News*, the *Arkansas Times*, *Quills and Pixels*, and *A Rough Sort of Beauty: Reflections on the Natural Heritage of Arkansas* (U of Arkansas Press 2002). She is co-author of *Under One Flag: A Year at Rohwer* by August House Publishing, a 2006 Historic Preservation Book Prize nominee.

Clint Stivers, originally from the beautiful state of Kentucky, is a PhD candidate at the University of Tennessee where he teaches cinema studies. He is currently writing a dissertation on the films of Terrence Malick.

Karley J. Sullivan graduated with a BFA from The University of Tennessee, Knoxville, in 2006. She grew up in a handmade house in South Knoxville and attended Laurel High School in Fort Sanders. She enjoys making art of all kinds.

Bob Thompson grew up in Kansas City. He lives in Fountain City despite his suspicion that the scarcity of sidewalks exacerbates his crotchety attitude toward automobiles (particularly a certain red SUV with a loud engine). He rides the bus downtown.

Emily Thompson grew up near Ann Arbor, Michigan, the place she will always consider home. She recently received her master's degree in fiction writing from the University of Tennessee. Her greatest joy is found in travel.

Bradford Tice received his MA in Poetry from the University of Colorado and is now at work on his PhD at the University of Tennessee in Knoxville. His poetry and fiction have appeared or are forthcoming in such periodicals as *The Atlantic Monthly, North American Review, Alaska Quarterly Review, Mississippi Review, Crab Orchard Review*, and the anthology *This New Breed: Gents, Bad Boys, and Barbarians 2* (Windstorm Creative). Brad would also like to thank the editors of the journal *Square One* in which his poem "Silicon" previously appeared.

Matt Urmy was born in New York City and raised in Tennessee. He continues to write poetry and songs and is currently living in Fort Sanders, Knoxville, Tennessee.

Carole Urmy is a writer and poet from Nashville, Tennessee. Her personal essays have appeared in *SUN* magazine and her poems have won awards in The Writers' Workshop contests in Asheville, North Carolina.

Jessica Weintraub is a third year PhD student at The University of Tennessee. She is interested in exploring science to find metaphors for human relationships. Her poems have appeared in *Poetry Scotland, in*tense*, and *New Millennium Writings*, and she won the Graduate Fiction Contest in 2005 for her story, "Base Pairs." Her article, "From AOK to Oz: The Historical Dictionary of American Slang," is forthcoming in *Discovering Popular Culture*. She is working on a novel for her dissertation.

Kory Wells' novel-in-progress *White Line to Graceville* was a finalist in the William Faulkner Competition. Her short fiction has appeared or is forthcoming in *Muscadine Lines: A Southern Anthology, Birmingham Arts Journal*, and other publications. A software developer, she writes about her desire to be an astronaut and living beyond traditional cultural roles in the anthology *She's Such a Geek* (Seal Press 2006). Although her body is succumbing to gravity and too many visits to the Dairy Queen, the native Tennessean is happiest when she prioritizes writing over exercise. Kory's mother, Judy Lee Green, also appears in this anthology. You may learn more about Kory at www.korywells.com.

Heather Wibbels received her BA in Philosophy and Religion from Transylvania University in Lexington, Kentucky, and then moved to Nashville where she received an MA in History and Critical Theories of Religion from Vanderbilt University. She has her own private practice as a massage therapist in Nashville and enjoys taking time out between clients to write. She completed the MTSU Writer's Loft program in April 2006 and won the Writer's Loft Literary Contest in the poetry category in the spring and fall of 2005. Wibbels agrees with Mark Doty's remark, "One of poetry's great powers is its preservative ability to take a moment in time and make an attempt to hold it," and strives to repeat it in her own writing.

Don Williams is a prize-winning columnist for *The Knoxville News-Sentinel*, www.knoxnews.com, www.OpedNews.com and other web outlets. He is also a freelance journalist, short story writer and the founding editor and publisher of *New Millennium Writings*, an annual anthology of fiction, nonfiction and poetry. His awards include a National Endowment for the Humanities Michigan Journalism Fellowship, a Golden Presscard Award and the Malcolm Law Journalism Prize. His short stories and magazine articles have been widely published, and he is finishing a novel, *Oracle of the Orchid Lounge*, set in his native Tennessee. He is the author of a book of journalism, *Heroes, Sheroes and Zeroes, Best Writings About People*. He is a founding member of the Knoxville Writers' Guild and also leads "Adventures in Writing" a creative writing workshop in Knoxville. For more information, email him at donwilliams7@charter.net. Or visit the NMW website at www.NewMillenniumWritings.com.

Melanie Williams is a student in Oak Ridge, Tennessee, and writes under the mentorship of Jane Sasser. Her poems have won some contests and awards.

Sylvia Woods is a native of Eastern Kentucky who grew up hearing the stories and songs of her people. She teaches high school English and lives in Oak Ridge, Tennessee. Her poetry has appeared in regional publications.

Marianne Worthington is a native of Knoxville, Tennessee. She is the author of *Larger Bodies Than Mine*, a poetry chapbook. She is the reviews editor for *Now & Then: The Appalachian Magazine*, a creative writing teacher for the Kentucky Governor's School for the Arts, and associate professor of communication arts at University of the Cumberlands, Williamsburg, Kentucky, where she teaches communication, media, and critical writing. Her memoir about growing up in Fountain City was included in *Knoxville Bound*, and her poems have appeared in *Shenandoah*, *Kalliope*, *Wind*, *The Louisville Review*, and in several anthologies.

Susan A. Wright is an assistant professor at Campbellsville University in Campbellsville, Kentucky. Her previous publications have been poetry, and she also will have an article in the upcoming *Gaming Lives in the 21st Century*. As someone who has loved to read and write since age eleven, Susan feels blessed to now be teaching writing, and she is currently finishing her doctorate in rhetoric and composition at the University of Louisville.

Index of Contributors

KNOXVILLE WRITERS' GUILD

Officers and Board of Directors
2006

RIP LYDICK, *president*

PAMELA SCHOENEWALDT, *vice-president*

JIM JOHNSTON, *treasurer*

ART STEWART, *secretary*

CAROLE BORGES, *membership*

PAM STRICKLAND, *publicity*

MARIANNE WORTHINGTON, *programming*

MARYBETH BOYANTON

REBECCA BROOKS

ALEX GABBARD

MARY BOZEMAN HODGES

RAINA KING

CANDANCE REAVES

JOHN REAVES